Sherman Takes Savannah

H. Ronald Freeman

Copyright © 2007 by H. Ronald Freeman

All rights reserved as to content and format. No part of this publication may be reproduced, stored in a retrieval system, or transmitted, in any form or by any means, electronic, mechanical, photocopying, recording, or otherwise, without the prior written permission of the publisher.

ISBN 0-9715274-2-3

Published by:
Freeport Publishing
Savannah, Georgia

Cover graphic design by Zachary Powers
Savannah, Georgia

Printed by Rose Printing Company
Tallahassee, Florida

Acknowledgments

Most books are conceived in the mind of an enthusiastic writer with reams of research ahead. Many times the writer assumes the reader has sat with him and absorbed all the terms and relationships and events that he has. Of course it isn't so. That's why most of us need someone to go over the amorphous mass of material and try to reformat it into some readable and understandable order.

For this task and her unwavering support and guidance I must give credit to my wife Judy who is practically a co-author of this book. Most of the material came from published sources that are readily accessible to the public. Sherman's army and its march through Georgia to the sea is a much told story. I only hope I have made it a little more concise and readable for those interested in Civil War history and Savannah as a major player in it.

Preface

Savannah was coming of age. Seventy-eight years had elapsed since the end of the Revolutionary War in which the town had been at the center of much of the action in the South. It had become a city of commerce, benefiting from the invention of the cotton gin by Eli Whitney at nearby Mulberry Grove plantation. Cotton had become the major industry not only in Savannah but the South.

The river teemed with trading vessels taking on cotton for English mills and bringing needed staples from European and Caribbean ports. Behind the commerce the city was sleepy and laid back in the southern tradition with its populace more interested in business than in politics. The planting of short staple cotton on inland plantations had brought the need of transportation and with it three major railroads connecting the port with points inland.

The city boasted four cotton compresses. These operations transformed the ginned cotton into tightly packed bales that had literally filled the river warehouses with the white gold. There were also iron foundries, sawmills, railroad shops and a rice mill. The key to the prosperity was, as from the outset, the lazy river that wound its way past the town to the sea, some 17 miles east.

Table of Contents

    Acknowledgments iii
    Preface iv
1. Secession 1
2. Fortification 10
3. Blockade 16
4. The Mosquito Fleet 22
5. Bartow 30
6. Ft. Pulaski 37
7. Bracing for Attack 52
8. Ft. McAllister 55
9. Town Without Pity 63
10. Sherman. 66
11 Atlanta to the Sea. 73
12. Lieutenants and Logistics 79
13. Marching Through Georgia 88
14. Push to Savannah 95
15. The Southern Alamo 103
16. The Noose Tightens 118
17. Yankees at the Gate 124
18. Battle Lines Drawn 136
19. Exodus 145
20. Surrender 153
21. 40 Acres and a Mule 165
22. Occupation 170
23. On to Carolina 188
24. Epilogue 198
    Savannah Map 205
    Illustration Credits 206
    Bibliography 209
    Chain of Command 211
    Index 212

Sherman Takes Savannah

Secession

It was the fall of 1861. There was tension everywhere. The air was electrified. Everyone seemed to feel the North and South were on a collision course from which neither side was able to veer. Commitments were being avowed and the time for argument was over. Minds would not be changed on either side. A line in the sand had been drawn.

National events, such as the publication of *Uncle Tom's Cabin* by Harriet Beecher Stowe in 1852, had further fanned the flames of abolitionism. The abolitionists in the North dug in and were determined to correct what they saw as a debasing of a person's inalienable right to freedom. Southerners, even those who owned no slaves, saw the North's position as meddling in affairs where they had no vested interest.

The Dred Scott decision by the U.S. Supreme Court in 1857 strengthened the southern argument by saying a slave was property and as such had no legal standing to sue for his freedom. The raiding party of John Brown of Kansas on the federal arsenal at Harper's Ferry in October 1859 showed the reaction from the northern side. Brown had hoped his raid would provoke an uprising of slaves and lead to an outbreak of war for freedom against slavery.

Col. Robert E. Lee, who was on extended leave from the army with his family in Virginia, was called on to lead the combined forces of militia and marines. He suppressed the raid and Brown was captured and convicted of treason against the United States for aggression against a federal property. He was hanged a few months later. The raid was a failure but his cause was burned into the minds of staunch abolitionists and Brown was thrust into the martyrdom he craved.

The Democratic National Convention had been held in Charleston in the fall of 1860. Paramount was the consideration of a presidential candidate but from the start there was a rift in the party concerning the stance on the slavery question. When

H. Ronald Freeman

the position arose in the party platform and the party refused to endorse slavery, the delegates from eight southern states walked out.

Historically the South had been dependent on the North for goods but now southern newspaper editorials were speaking out against that dependency. They spoke of the need for an independent South whether they were forced into it by federal pressure or acted on their own initiative.

Abraham Lincoln, of the new Republican Party, was already being touted as the abolitionist candidate. To many, he represented the end to private property, states' rights and their personal freedom.

After the presidential election in 1860 the rallies in Savannah went on nightly, aided by bonfires, torches and parades of banners. Johnson Square was often the site of these impromptu rallies. Gifted speakers whipped the crowds to frenzy with rabid talk of Yankee tyranny. Savannah audiences were targeted with speech after speech.

Johnson Square Oratory

Torches burned in the squares as the oratory of secession inflamed the already heated passions for war. To those in the South it all came down to the matter of states' rights and the fact that the federal government

Sherman Takes Savannah

was meddling in states' affairs. Obviously the direct question before them was slavery but the greater question was which government, federal or state, had the utmost dominion in the matter. The question had united most of the whites in Savannah on the side of states' rights. It had also united most of the blacks, although on a different side entirely.

One of the most outspoken and gifted of the orators on the side of states' rights was 44-year old Francis Bartow, a Savannah attorney. Born in Savannah, the son of a respected physician, he went on to graduate from Yale Law School and return to Savannah to marry the daughter of Senator John Macpherson Berrien. He was an experienced and persuasive trial lawyer whose noted successes before many a jury enabled him to express his positions with an admirable eloquence.

The election of Abraham Lincoln as president only served to inflame the town more. It was no longer a question of whether the town would object or submit to what it felt represented an oppressive administration; it was just a matter of how they would resist.

The Georgia General Assembly took a leap forward to hostility when it voted to appropriate a million dollars for the defense of the state. It also named Henry C. Wayne of Savannah, the son of Supreme Court Justice James Wayne, to the newly created position of Adjutant and Inspector General. Wayne readily accepted the call knowing he couldn't turn his back on his homeland. In so doing he became the first Georgian to respond to the call of his state. He had spent twenty years in the army since his 1838 graduation from West Point. His father agreed with his decision although he personally chose to remain a member of the federal court.

Vocal leaders in Savannah expressed their opinions that any dissolution of the Union was due to the violation of the law on the part of the northern legislature rather than any action from southern representatives. Any cleavage in the Union would be placed squarely on northern shoulders.

H. Ronald Freeman

In the mind of the white southern male it was impossible to disassociate the new Republican Party with that of a black influenced government. Even those southerners who had been staunch Unionists for most of their lives now felt the change being imposed upon them. They felt they were being forced into a future where they would be subjugated to the black race.

The white churches began falling in line. Ministers were siding with the sentiments of their congregations. A bishop in the Catholic Church had blamed the northern Protestant ministers for inflaming the current feelings in the North. Secret societies were already being formed in Savannah and initiating a reign of terror for those who even alluded to Union sympathies.

As expected and predicted, Lincoln had been elected with only forty percent of the popular vote. In Savannah, as in most southern cities, the people accepted the fact. They had already disassociated themselves from the country and because of that could not be expected to be overwhelmed in one way or the other. A public hearing was held in Savannah and a resolution passed not recognizing Lincoln's election. This in turn was forwarded to the state legislature.

Bear in mind that Lincoln was only elected in early November. By December 21st, the Georgia General Assembly passed an act acknowledging a crisis in the government on a national basis and provided that delegates be elected to a state convention to consider measures to be taken and even resistance if suitable.

The town was in an absolute frenzy. Demonstrations were everywhere. Secession was the talk of the day. Georgia talked, but South Carolina acted by seceding from the Union on December 20th. Prominent Carolina statesmen commented to Georgia's Gov. Joseph Brown that Carolina had acted with boldness and purpose and hopefully Georgia would also show her alliance with her sister in the South.

Savannah celebrated South Carolina's action with demonstrations and torch parades. The whole city was

Sherman Takes Savannah

illuminated on the night of December 26th. In Georgia it was almost a fait accompli.

As a countermove for defense, U. S. troops stationed in Charleston, evacuated Ft. Moultrie and moved to Ft. Sumter where they felt they stood a better chance of defending if necessary. Leaders in Georgia felt Ft. Pulaski in Savannah could be in danger of federal seizure if not taken under southern custody immediately.

The elected convention of Georgia met in Milledgeville on January 16th. Alabama had seceded on the 12th. As stated in the Savannah Morning News, "the only question now was what would constitute the northern boundary of the new nation." The delegation from Savannah voted at each roll call to leave the Union. Mississippi, Florida and Alabama had already followed South Carolina's lead in secession and Georgia joined them on January 19th. On February 1st, the new Georgia flag was unfurled over the U.S. Custom House in Savannah. It was all becoming unraveled on a too-quick basis.

Gov. Joseph Brown

Shortly after the State held its election of delegates, Gov. Joseph Brown was called to Savannah from the capital at Milledgeville due to a warning from Sen. Toombs in Washington that Ft. Pulaski was in danger of being occupied by federal troops.

Gov. Brown had been requested by Col. Lawton to come and take control of the city as commander of the state troops in Savannah. The governor, after conferring with

H. Ronald Freeman

Lawton, Wayne and other city leaders ordered the first hostile action of what was to become the Civil War, the immediate capture of Ft. Pulaski.

Lawton commanded the First Volunteer Regiment of Georgia that was composed of the nine original volunteer companies in Savannah.

Lawton was ordered by the governor to take possession of the fort and to hold it until he received orders to the contrary personally or a superior force overpowered him. Gov. Brown sent telegrams to his sister states of Alabama, Louisiana, Florida and Mississippi informing them of his coming action.

Lawton had military training, being in the class of 1839 at West Point. He had gone on to Harvard Law School and was a practicing attorney in Savannah as well as a state senator and the president of the Augusta & Savannah Railroad.

Alexander Lawton

Not wishing to head pell-mell into a fortified situation, Gov. Brown had dispatched a scout to reconnoiter the fort and assess its defense. Henry Rootes Jackson, a Savannahian, had been chosen for the assignment. He was a practicing attorney in town and a native of Athens. His background was both colorful and full. He had served as a minister to Austria, a newspaper editor, superior court judge and a colonel in the Mexican War of a Georgia volunteer regiment. Jackson headed downriver in a rowboat in the rain and found Pulaski to be undefended and staffed only by custodians.

Sherman Takes Savannah

Brown's plan was not to be carried out with stealth; it was even written up in the newspaper that the fort was to be seized. According to advertised plan, 134 men and six artillery pieces boarded the steamer *Ida* and set forth downriver to carry out Gov. Brown's order. The men were from the companies of the Chatham Artillery, the Savannah Volunteer Guards and the Oglethorpe Light Infantry. Well-wishers thronged the docks and made it difficult for the boarding party to even move about. Practically the entire town turned out to see them off and many felt this was the beginning of what would be told in years to come as a glorious beginning of a new nation.

The militia arrived and was able to move in the fort without firing a single shot. It was the first hostile action of the war happening three months prior to the firing on Ft. Sumter in Charleston.

Pulaski had been in a caretaker status and much would need to be done to transform the neglected assemblage of bricks into a fortress to be reckoned with. The guns were rusting and resting on carriages that were rotting and the parade ground for the most part was overgrown.

Actually, it was a delicate situation. At the time of seizure the state of Georgia was still a member of the Union and therefore Ft. Pulaski was still the property of the United States. Nevertheless, Gov. Brown ordered Col. Charles Olmstead to take possession of the fort for the state. This action, to date, was the most hostile by any southern state against the Union up to this time.

To set things in perspective though, as mentioned previously, Ft. Pulaski had been in a caretaker status by the federal government and the only federal occupants were an ordinance sergeant and a caretaker. The officer in charge was away at the time. Upon his return he arrived at the fort and was received with great civility by Col. Lawton.

Lawton further advised the officer, Capt. Whiting, to close up his business with the U.S. Army. Whiting obliged and being Mississippi born, soon accepted a commission in the Provisional Army of the Confederacy.

In March, the State Convention met again, this time in Savannah. Alexander H. Stephens, Vice President of the Confederacy, gave what was to be termed the "Cornerstone Speech." In essence his cornerstone rested on the premise that the black man was not the equal of the white man; and slavery, merely the blacks' subordination to a superior race, was a natural and normal condition.

Alexander Stephens

During this period of dissension there were several cases of punch and counterpunch between the two opposing sides. New York City had seized several cases of guns purchased for the State of Georgia by Gazaway B. Lamar, a southern banker residing in the north. In return, Gov. Brown ordered the seizure of all vessels in Savannah owned by citizens of New York.

It was the portent of things to come. In the next month, on April 12, 1861, Ft. Sumter in Charleston received its first shelling. The south was jubilant at the news. Most felt God was on their side and regardless of the length of time it would take, the North would learn its lesson and meanwhile God would defend the South.

When news of the fall of Fort Sumter reached the legislators in Atlanta, many implored their fellow

Sherman Takes Savannah

representatives to cease all talk of cooperation and listen to the thunder of cannon and rifle fire along with the clash of sabers from their committed neighbors in South Carolina. The emotion was there and to the calculated question of, "Will they have to go it alone," came the expected answer in unison of, "No, never!"

For cooler heads in Savannah supporting the preservation of the Union, the only way to express their dismay was to stay away from the polls in the election of delegates to the state convention. It was to no avail. The die had been cast. The Rubicon had been crossed.

Episcopal Bishop Stephen Elliott, a political force in Savannah was nimble in verbally coming to the aid of his southern constituents. He was handsome, physically attractive and an accomplished and eloquent speaker. Elliott saw the question as a turn away from the core of republicanism, the premise on which the country was founded. At its core, the argument of the North was flawed and the South was justified in defending the existing order and Christian principles.

After listening and reacting, Georgia acted. The time for talking was over. Secession was a fait accompli and each state in the South knew the North would not permit dissolution of the Union. The southern attitude was "Let the chips fall where they may."

H. Ronald Freeman

Fortification

The city fathers were aware of their exposure to attack. A militia needed to be armed and the city fortified. They knew the grace period would be short and it was imperative that they be ready. Francis Bartow, a Savannah attorney, was now Chairman of the Military Affairs Committee of the Provisional Congress of the Confederate States. During the meetings in Montgomery, Alabama, he expressed his concerns about military preparedness to Col. Alexander Lawton back in Savannah. How much powder and shot were on hand and what resources and facilities did the state have for producing more?

Most southern leaders knew they were grossly unprepared in the event of a war. Even in Savannah, where there were nine volunteer companies making up the 1st Volunteer Regiment of Georgia commanded by Col. Lawton, there was a general lack of readiness.

Troops shipping out to Va. in 1861

To prepare themselves a determined effort and a push was begun to transition the peacetime soldiers into an effective war machine. Many of the handsome dress uniforms used for parades were being replaced by those more functional in the

Sherman Takes Savannah

field. The Savannah Volunteer Guards had chosen a coarse gray cloth for their field wear. It was snappy and Bartow so admired this uniform that he insisted that Congress prescribe this gray for the official uniform of the Confederate States Army. At the outbreak of war there was no standard for uniforms as to color or style. The uniform was approved and the rest is history. Thus began the saga of the blue versus the gray.

To display its military might to the community, the 1st Regiment paraded with their assembled one thousand men through the Savannah streets. It was a show in numbers only since there was little organization or structured leadership for the militia. They were still waiting for a general officer of the army to be assigned to command the defenses in the area. Everyone was anxious about the exposure of Ft. Pulaski. Since being seized by the state in January it still had not been turned over to the new Confederate government.

Finally, in April the government did act and commissioned Col. Lawton a brigadier general to command the district. This only added to the feeling of anticipation and excitement in the air.

Actually Ft. Pulaski had been teeming with activity since its seizure. Slaves on loan from planters on the surrounding farms had dug out the moats and cleared them of mud. The entire 650-man garrison was engaged in laying sandbags, stocking the provisions of the fort and installing the large guns and tracks necessary for her defense.

Where was the enemy? Did the one hundred and twenty-eight pound cannonball of the fort's largest cannon intimidate them? Certainly, northern vessels would need to take notice. The men knew they were equal to a whole fleet of enemy vessels heading up the river. To a man they were willing to defend Pulaski under fire and stand behind their guns. Tybee Island was only a mile east of the fort and a lone battery along with a small contingent of troops defended it. As one could imagine, in the summer it was a pleasant place to be. Balmy ocean breezes and white sandy beaches made it hard for the troops to believe they were there for other than recreational purposes. On the western side of Ft. Pulaski, about eight miles upriver and on the same side stood Ft.

Coastal Savannah Area

Jackson. It was also garrisoned to thwart any federal occupation that could sever communication with the city.

Sherman Takes Savannah

The Savannah River was the primary stream but there were other waterways into the city as well. One was the Wilmington River entered from south of Tybee Island and back into the Savannah River about four miles east of the city and east of Ft. Jackson as well. To protect the Wilmington River a battery was erected on the beach at the north end of Warsaw Island, below Tybee, and an added one at Thunderbolt, about four and a half miles southeast of the city.

Another approach into the city was the Vernon River from Ossabaw Sound which flowed into the Wilmington River. To fortify that route, a battery was placed on Green Island in the Ossabaw Sound. This was accomplished primarily by slave labor.

In addition to those three vulnerable waterways into the city, the Ogeechee River, south of the city, flowed into the Ossabaw Sound. A vital railhead about 12 miles south of Savannah was also served by the Ogeechee. To protect this railhead, a fortification called Ft. McAllister was begun a few miles downstream.

As the coastal batteries grew in number, the public became more and more confident that no enemy vessel would be able to breach the defenses or land a party of federal troops on their beaches.

Protecting the coast was one thing, but another was the matter of the navy itself. The Confederate States were bordered by an extensive coastline but had nothing anywhere close to resembling a navy. It wasn't due to lack of talent since many of the U.S. Naval officers, just as their army brethren, had resigned their commissions to come home and defend their southern heritage.

Among these and the most prominent was Josiah Tattnall, son of one of the early governors of Georgia and a native of Savannah. Tattnall was now sixty-five years of age and had served the U.S. Navy for the last forty-eight of them. During his service in China in 1859 he had gained international

H. Ronald Freeman

notoriety by coining the phrase, "blood is thicker than water." This was said in reference to his going to the aid of a British ship under attack in Asian waters.   Like his fellow officers, Tattnall faced a difficult choice. He had expressed himself earlier as being a staunch supporter of the Union but at the same time knew he couldn't go against the state of his birth. Tattnall made his choice but was assailed in the North for it.

Tattnall was commissioned as the Senior Flag Officer of the Georgia Navy. It was an interesting command as well as a challenging one since the State of Georgia possessed no ships. Even though Adjutant General Wayne and his agents had attempted to purchase schooners and steamers in the North, they were unsuccessful. This meant there were no ships available to the South. And without the purchase, the South was bereft of a navy.

Commodore Josiah Tattnall. III

Finally, they succeeded in purchasing the *Everglade*, a paddle wheeler that would be outfitted with two smoothbore cannon. She was 122 feet in length and had plied the inland waters as a passenger steamer and she was currently berthed In Savannah. Her only boast was that of an elegant main salon in the fashion of many of the riverboats of the day.   She was renamed the *Savannah* and became the flagship of the Georgia Navy with her officers and crew numbering sixty-one men.

The charge of the *Savannah* was to cruise from the Savannah River as far south as the St. Mary's River that bordered Florida. The general feeling to observers was that

Sherman Takes Savannah

the ship was absurd but her sister ships in the squadron were even more so. Two old tugboats were converted into warships by the addition of a cannon mounted to each of their decks. They were joined by another side-wheeler with a deck-mounted boiler and engine. Such was the Georgia navy to the consternation and indignity of Tattnall.

Tattnall had confided to William Russell, the British correspondent, that "I have no fleet. Long before the Southern Confederacy has a fleet that can cope with the stars and stripes, my bones will be white in the grave."

Tattnall, like many other officers from both ranks of service, had seen the other side. He knew the depth of men and munitions the North could bring to bear against them. He knew the bravado expressed on the part of southern leaders and politicians would need to be backed with something other than threats. Munitions and equipment were needed immediately and the South had little in the way of capital or credit to pay for them. At this point there was no South, only a loose confederation of independent states that were just as unwilling to cooperate with each other as they were with their former allegiance to the Union.

H. Ronald Freeman

Blockade

It was a simple matter. The North had the ships and the South did not. Plus, the South had hundreds of miles of exposed coastline that it depended on for goods and munitions and the Union wanted it sealed up tight.

The State of Georgia had only a few dilapidated boats that had been converted into gun-ships, whereas the North seemed to possess an endless armada made up of gunboats, frigates, sloops of war, troop transports and coal transports. They sent 79 of these vessels transporting 12,000 troops to establish a blockade along the coasts of Georgia and South Carolina. It was the most powerful armada assembled in America up to that point.

The Union boats converged on Hilton Head Island on Port Royal Sound, South Carolina as a homeport. The problem was that it was only 25 miles north of Savannah and was still

Savannah Evacuates

Sherman Takes Savannah

occupied by southern forces. As it turned out it was not a problem and by November 1861 the Union would administer an elementary lesson in naval warfare to the South. The fort was quickly reduced to rubble by repeated cannon fire. Fort Walker at Port Royal quickly succumbed. There was never a doubt. Confederate artillery fire was wretched and scored only a few holes in Union ships with eight seamen killed and six wounded. The southern gunners were so inept they permitted their 8, 10 and 11-inch guns to recoil and slip from their mounts.

Gen. Robert E. Lee

When Savannah residents heard about the defeat of Port Royal there was the expected pandemonium. Outgoing trains were packed with women and children bound for the interior. Citizens thronged the streets near the newspaper and telegraph offices for the latest news. The town quickly became deserted.

On the heels of this disaster, Gen. Robert E. Lee immediately assumed command of the Military Department of Georgia, South Carolina and Florida. At once he set out to inspect the coastal defenses from Savannah to as far south as Amelia Island off the coast of north Florida. His findings verified their condition as poor indeed.

H. Ronald Freeman

To a newly formed army very taken with its appearance and dress, Lee was an enigma. He was very unassuming in his uniform and was described by observers as plainly clothed while the other generals in his command dressed within an inch of their lives with military regalia. In physical appearance, he was tall in stature with an erect posture, graceful movements and hair just beginning to be touched with gray. His facial expression was one of reserve and resolve. It was during his stay in Savannah that he purchased a handsome gray steed named Greenbrier that would take him to many places and battles during the next four years. Lee renamed his warhorse Traveller.

He had been given the charge of about 300 miles of coastline staffed with poorly armed and poorly trained troops, only a few guns, poor communications and a total Union blockade offshore that was containing them. He had to draw heavily on his education in military engineering and command of scarce resources. He knew the utmost priority would be consolidating the isolated units up and down the coast.

To accomplish this Lee ordered the garrisons from exposed positions evacuated. This left a large expanse of the coast abandoned. Confederate troops on Tybee Island were withdrawn and this didn't go unnoticed by the Union blockade. Before long, Union troops made a landing on the island. On November 24, 1861, three Union gunboats began bombarding Tybee Island and drove off the remnants of rebel forces. The following day, federal forces came ashore unopposed and planted the Union flag. Many fires were lit for the evening to give the rebels the impression that they had arrived in force.

Southern troops watched from Ft. Pulaski, little realizing that the foothold on Tybee would later become the key to reducing the fort they were defending. Its occupation also effectively shut down any exit by boats attempting to leave the city via the Savannah River due to the presence of federal gunboats.

Sherman Takes Savannah

Federal commander Samuel Francis Dupont observed that with the fall of Tybee Island, it was only a matter of time before Pulaski would fall, given its close proximity to the island.

Dupont's summation of the situation was that "With Tybee's capture, Savannah is completely stopped up." A *New York Tribune* reporter agreed and added that "the city is at our mercy." The *New York Herald* responded, "Henceforth, Savannah is of no importance to the South as a port." Dupont obviously agreed since his ships denied the Atlantic totally to Savannah.

At this point federal gunboats blocked the mouth of the Savannah River at Tybee Roads, the main entrance into the Savannah River. In a few days they also controlled Warsaw Island south of Tybee and the mouth of the Wilmington River. Confederate troops in their forts and batteries could do nothing - only watch and wait.

Military leaders in the South now realized their efforts in fortifying the coast had been no more than costly experiments and a waste of time. Occupying the coastal islands required the deployment of too many men that were critically needed elsewhere. All that could be done was for Commodore Tattnall and his "mosquito fleet" to cruise down the Savannah River to its mouth, being visible and firing a few shots at the federal gunboats while under the protection of Ft. Pulaski.

It was only a matter of months before the Union boats were able to open a passage to the Savannah River from the sound and only a few miles upriver from Ft. Pulaski thus totally skirting the fort. For this purpose they used Wall's Cut, an old but relatively unknown waterway from South Carolina. Wilmington Island east of the town was evacuated and federal troops severed the telegraph line between Ft. Pulaski and Savannah. This terminated communication between the town and the fort.

Union troops erected batteries at three points on the river between Savannah and Ft. Pulaski and made reprovisioning of the fort virtually impossible. The clock on Pulaski had begun to tick.

From the southern side there was a strong sentiment that a force should be mounted to wrest control of the coastal islands from Union troops. This idea did not go far. Although no one liked the idea of Yankees at their doorstep, the feeling was why go to the great expense of driving the enemy from a position that once taken could not be held.

Citizens of Savannah expected a federal attack at any moment. If it turned into a reality, many thought the smoldering ashes of their once proud city should greet the Union forces. But finally, cooler heads prevailed. They knew torching the town would produce no serious disadvantage to the enemy but that it would inflict a stupendous injury to the city and the state.

On the other side there was hesitancy on the part of Union commanders. They were convinced that a force nearing 65,000 troops was in defense of Savannah. Also, while they had the option of steaming up the river and laying siege to the town, they thought a better and safer approach would be to attack a more visible target. Ft. Pulaski was the obvious choice and was still there to be taken.

Union naval officers had boasted Savannah could be sealed from incoming and outgoing river traffic by placing a frigate in the channel to Tybee Island and out of range of Pulaski's guns. This was easily accomplished and even southern naval officers had to agree that no part of the Atlantic coast had been more effectively sealed than the port of Savannah.

By the summer of 1861 the coils of the blockade were slowly tightening around the town. Still, it was possible for some of the more elusive blockade-runners to slip in and out and never be spotted by a Union ship. Greatly assisting these boats was the fact that Great Britain was a southern sympathizer and made their ports in Bermuda and the Bahamas available for refueling and provisioning. The

Sherman Takes Savannah

blockade-runners though would find that the window for this activity would be soon closed.

The change came with the fall of Port Royal and with it the ability of Union boats to dock there as a home base, deploying their boats along the Georgia and South Carolina coasts. The tightening blockade did more to hurt Savannah than anything before the coming of Sherman. Admiral Dupont, in charge of the Union blockade around Savannah said, "I will cork up Savannah like a bottle."

Was it beginning to dawn on at least the small part of the population of the South represented by Savannah that at least by water, they were overpowered? The enemy was stationed only a few miles from their doorstep and had overrun that position with ease and it was still early in the war. Perhaps hope was vested in ground forces opposing what was felt to be inferior troops from the North. And after all, wasn't God on their side?

H. Ronald Freeman

The Mosquito Fleet

Savannah led the South in the building of vessels for the southern cause. All in all, three ironclads were constructed: the *Georgia,* the *Atlanta* and the *Savannah.* There were also several other boats that were converted to gunboats or ironclads and assembled in Savannah.

The *CSS Georgia,* launched in May 1862, can only be described as floating hulk. She was coated with four inches of armor plating forged from 500 tons of railroad iron. She stretched 250 feet in overall length and carried ten heavy guns. The workmen started with an old barge and built onto it a

C.S.S. Georgia

thick wooden gun deck, sloped to deflect enemy shot. The construction of the *Georgia* was by trial-and-error overseen by people with little shipbuilding experience. No plans, drawings, or records of the ironclad's construction have ever surfaced.

She was so dysfunctional she was almost a mutant. Her engines were too small to propel her forward against the

Sherman Takes Savannah

current and she could only move with the assistance of a small armada of towboats moving her into whatever position she was to occupy. As if lack of mobility wasn't enough of a hindrance, then there were the leaks, not only from the hull but above as well. When it rained there was not a dry spot in quarters below including the bunks where the seamen slept. She sported several names, all of which were uncomplimentary. Included in her monikers were "Mud Tub", "Splendid Failure" and even "Iron Box" since she was not a boat but a floating battery. The *Georgia* was placed in a special location in the Savannah River near Fort Jackson where she could be turned to direct a barrage to either the north or south channel.

    The *Atlanta* was another story entirely and was the South's most powerful armored vessel. She was formerly a blockade-runner named the *Fingal* and her subsequent conversion was almost total. Everything about her was modified with the exception of her lower hull and British engine. She was 204-feet long and wielded a twenty-foot iron prod with a star torpedo at her bow. She cruised at seven knots and

CSS Atlanta

drew sixteen feet, definitely a hindrance in Savannah's shallow coastal waters. Due to an unventilated hold, the crew slept in a

H. Ronald Freeman

tender behind the boat. She was coated with four inches of railroad iron and her armament included seven-inch Brooke rifles at her bow and stern and with a six-inch Brooke on each side.

Because of the *Atlanta's* strong engine she was considered more formidable than the famous *Merrimac* and greatly respected by the federal navy. She was commissioned early in 1863. When she made her first voyage down the Savannah River toward Ft. Pulaski, the federals that saw her became quite nervous. They felt that now their smaller Union gunboats would know what it was like to be blown out of the water. What they didn't know was the *Atlanta* had poor helm response, too deep a draft for coastal waters and leaked continually.

And then there was the *Savannah.* She was a steam sloop commissioned in the summer of 1863. She was 174 feet long and 45 feet wide and drew twelve and a half feet of water. She was armed with five rifled guns and her engines and boilers were constructed at the Columbus Naval Iron Works in west Georgia. Her crew consisted of 27 officers and 154 men. Even Commodore Tattnall called her, "a well-constructed and very fine ship." She was armed with four Brooke 6.4 inch guns, a ram and a torpedo.

The crew disagreed with Tattnall's assessment. They felt the *Savannah* was a floating sieve and a miserable ship on which to live and work. Although it was impervious to enemy shells, the plating denied the men below deck both light and ventilation. Given the stifling Savannah heat and humidity, survival below was nearly impossible. The ironclad was so hot that the crew, like on her sister ship the *Atlanta,* was allowed to sleep on a tender. As expected, there were deserters. Those who swam to Ft. Pulaski were described as being very unhappy with conditions aboard. A crewman wrote, "no one in the world could tell me whether it was day or night if he had no means of marking time. I would venture if a person were blindfolded and carried below deck and

Sherman Takes Savannah

turned loose he would believe himself in a swamp, for the water is trickling in all the time and it is totally damp."

Southern naval officers received much criticism because of their reluctance to pit the *Atlanta* and her sister ironclads against the northern monitors that were patrolling Savannah's coast. Much of this was directed at Tattnall who was leery of the ironclads and planned his attacks only when they were absent in the vicinity. He was willing to attack the Union's wooden gunboats at Ft. McAllister but only when the ironclads were elsewhere. His studied opinion was that the *Atlanta* wasn't maneuverable enough around the coastal shoals to take on the iron monitors from the North.

The Confederate Navy received much criticism too from southern newspapers. They were incensed at Tattnall's meekness and demanded he be replaced with someone who would take an offensive stance against the Union blockade. Many felt he was not aggressive enough to command Georgia's naval operations. Subsequently, he was replaced in March 1862.

After leaving Savannah Tattnall was given the command of the James River Squadron and charged with defending the waters near Norfolk. On his flagship, the *CSS Virginia (formerly the USS Merrimac),* he engaged the *Monitor* a second time, after the classic encounter at Hampton Roads, but again with negligible results. When the Southern forces withdrew from Norfolk, he was forced to scuttle the *Virginia* since her deep draft would not be navigable in the coastal waters. This action, similar to his inaction in Savannah, didn't play well with the media or in other vocal quarters. Tattnall's position was that he didn't have many options. It was either scuttle the boat or leave it to fall in enemy hands. He demanded a court martial to clear his name. When the obvious facts were presented, he was acquitted of any dereliction of duty.

H. Ronald Freeman

The southern populace however would not let it rest. They didn't care that a lack of action would let the boat fall into Yankee hands. General criticism was that Tattnall was too old for active duty and was resting on his laurels. Increasingly, he came under public pressure to use his boats to attack the North. Again, in March 1863 as before in Savannah, he was relieved of his active command and reassigned to command the Savannah naval station. It was a desk job and shore duty at its worst.

Tattnall's immediate successor, Richard L. Page, lasted only a month. He was a first cousin to Robert E. Lee but like Tattnall, he lacked the aggression to satisfy his superiors. During his month of command, the *Atlanta* was experiencing steering problems but his superiors thought it was a very poor excuse. Enter William A. Webb who had been captain of a gunboat at Hampton Roads during the battle of the *Monitor* and *Merrimac* and had impressed some of his fellow officers as being young and daring and full of pluck. Those not in his camp of admirers sized him up as impetuous, reckless and unwilling to listen to older and more experienced officers.

There were other experienced naval officers who were realistic in their assessment of the *Atlanta* and warned against over optimism. It was pointed out that her officers were inexperienced and the most of the crew were not seasoned sailors. In addition, her hull was suspect due to the added weight.

Webb saw none of this and revealed his plans to clear the blockade of ironclads. Once that was accomplished he would attack the shipping at Port Royal and finally cut the cord to sever Ft. Pulaski, now in Union hands, from its supplies. Some felt he should wait for the launching of the *Savannah*, now nearly ready for service. Webb turned a deaf ear and said, "the whole abolition fleet holds no terror for me." He planned to attack the Union blockade post haste.

Union fleet commanders heard of Webb's plans through deserters and dispatched the monitors *Weehawken* and

Sherman Takes Savannah

Nahunt to Warsaw Island where the Wilmington River emptied into the Atlantic. Learning this, Webb decided to stay within the sound to deal with the ironclads. He felt the chance of a lifetime had been dropped in his lap. He would become famous. At last the *Atlanta* was being given the chance to show what she could do. Webb, as captain, felt she also finally had the commander to take her through her paces.

Early the next morning, June 16th, after taking on more coal that deepened her draft even further, the commander felt the *Atlanta* was ready. She steamed out and at 4:10 a.m. was spotted by the *Weehawken.* Soon the *Nahunt* joined in the hunt. Undeterred, the *Atlanta* plowed proudly on, the pride of the Confederacy, ready to blow the Yankees into submission and make them pay for past humiliations. The order was given for full steam ahead and the *Atlanta* entered the sound. Webb's plan was ambitious; to take on both ironclads at once. The first encountered would be rammed and destroyed with the spar torpedo and the other would be finished off with the guns in the classic manner.

Like many well-made plans, it was not to be. With the increased weight and draft she ran aground on a sandbar just after entering the sound and was unable to free herself. Not only that but she was listing so badly that her guns could not be brought to bear on the enemy monitors.

The northern boats noted her predicament and moved in like wolves to the kill. At six hundred yards the *Atlanta* sent a shot from her bow gun hoping to make the Union boats engage at a distance. It splashed between the monitors. They weren't fooled and continued to close. The *Weehawken* held her fire and deliberately stalked to three hundred yards then fired her fifteen-inch gun. The huge solid shot, propelled by thirty pounds of powder, smashed into the *Atlanta's* side and dislodged large iron and wooden splinters from the bulkhead, wounding sixteen men and rendering forty senseless from concussion. The impact drove the *Atlanta's* shells out of their racks, adding to the destruction. An eleven-inch shell followed, crashing into the lightly armored knuckles. The *Atlanta i*mmediately sprung a serious leak. A third shot struck a gun shutter as it was attempting to fire, wounding half the gun crew. While still reeling from that she was hit again. This time demolishing the wheelhouse and wounding the pilots and helmsman.

*Now the *Atlanta* was truly helpless. She had no mobility of movement and was unable to train her guns on the enemy boats. She was not engaging but only enduring. The *Atlanta* was lock-step to destruction and it was only a matter of time. Just 20 minutes into the battle and Webb was forced to surrender his vessel and his crew of 137 men. He had gotten off only seven badly aimed shots that failed to strike anything and the *Nahunt* was pounding up to join the *Weehawken* in battle. Ignominious in defeat, they were sent north to a prison compound in New York harbor at Ft. Lafayette.

The Savannah community along with the entire South received the news in disbelief. They had anticipated a brilliant victory but again had to reconcile themselves to the demonstrated ineptness on the part of their shipbuilders and navy. The *Atlanta* was repaired by the Union navy at Port Royal and refitted at the naval yard Philadelphia. From there she continued in the service of the Union and was cited for her actions in destroying Confederate rams in the James River in the final push by Grant's army to capture Richmond.

Construction on the southern ironclads was slowed by a lack of iron plating and engine parts, problems that plagued the entire Confederate navy. Most of the armor consisted of flattened rails bolted to a thick backing of oak and pine. The propulsion machinery, which was manufactured in Columbus, Georgia, was generally of good quality but it proved inadequate to move such massive ships. Although failures at their intended purpose, the presence of the ironclads was a serious deterrent to Union forays.

Sherman Takes Savannah

Even if the ironclads had been fit for extensive travel, they would have been hampered by a chronic lack of fuel. Only forty-five coal cars were available to support the needs of ships at Charleston, Savannah, and Columbus, where nine ironclads and numerous smaller vessels eventually were in operation.

Because the ships were constructed with green timber and caulked with cotton, they suffered severe leakage problems, and pumps operated continuously to keep them afloat.

After the *Atlanta's* embarrassing encounter in Warsaw Sound it all fell to the *Savannah* to uphold southern honor. She was commanded by William W. Hunter and was considered a powerful vessel. The problem was the blockade had grown ever tighter; and with evidence of the *Atlanta's* fighting ability before them, Confederate naval officials refused to sacrifice the *Savannah* and send her out to battle.

The ships, like the town, were bottled up. Tattnall realized this but voicing that opinion was quite unpopular with both the southern press and the Confederate naval department. The best the "mosquito fleet" could hope for was to keep the Union gunboats and ironclads out of their waters. The most effective way to accomplish that was by placing mines in the local rivers. This was very effective but was also a double-edged sword. The mines kept the northern boats out but they also kept the southern boats in.

H. Ronald Freeman

Bartow

    A line in the sand had been drawn and it was not the Mason-Dixon but the adjoining borders of Virginia, Maryland and Washington, D.C. Both sides were scurrying about equipping and training their armies to take the field against each other for the first time. Everyone felt the scene of the action would be near the nation's capital. All of Savannah's military units wanted to be there when the shooting started but Gov. Brown had other ideas. He was determined to keep all the troops in and near Savannah for the protection of the city and the coast.
    In the minds of most of the men in Savannah, that was no way to fight a war. It was obvious to them that they were needed where the action was. Many of the militia units in the state were losing men to desertion from those hustling to Virginia to join other units. Gov. Brown came down hard on this and insisted that their equipment belonged to the State of Georgia. This meant if they chose to go, it was at their own expense.
    Capt. Francis S. Bartow was determined to take his company, the Oglethorpe Light Infantry, to the front. They would not be left to languish in what he termed the "inglorious ease" of staying at home. This is what Gov. Brown had ordered for Savannah militia units. The governor wanted Georgia troops at home defending Georgia soil.
    Although Georgia and other southern states refused to allow the Confederacy to control their militia, the Confederate Congress authorized President Davis to accept service when offered by independent units that were smaller than regiment size. Upon hearing this, Bartow acted immediately and telegraphed the news to Savannah from Montgomery. The Oglethorpe Light Infantry met that same evening and voted unanimously to offer their service to the Confederacy. They dispatched a telegram to Bartow of their decision, which he

Sherman Takes Savannah

then delivered personally to Jefferson Davis, who accepted their offer graciously and immediately.

Gov. Brown repeated his order that no unit would take arms, munitions or other state property beyond Georgia borders without his consent. Bartow ignored the order and informed Brown that he was under orders from the President of the Confederate States. "I go to illustrate my native state," said Bartow, and asked for the blessings and commendations of everyone in Georgia.

The unit was given an enthusiastic sendoff at the Central Railway depot. A band was playing and a flag that had been made by local ladies was presented to the outfit. Bartow told the ladies that if the flag was not returned it would be because not one arm was left in the unit to bear it aloft. There was no way they could know the truth and prophesy of that statement in the weeks, months and years to come. The unit's historian would write in later years that

Francis S. Bartow

the Oglethorpe Light Infantry left their dead and wounded on almost every battlefield from the opening at Bull Run to the closing at Appomattox four years later.

Even as he left Georgia, Bartow was not allowed to escape the wrath of Gov. Brown. The governor dashed off a

H. Ronald Freeman

scathing and accusing letter to instill in him a feeling of guilt for leaving the city undefended while going to the front where it was doubtful he was really needed. Given their history it was no surprise that the letter struck a nerve in Bartow. Although time was short and he felt little inclination to reply, he did. Bartow responded to Brown in a long letter that his first commitment was to his country and for that gubernatorial permission was not needed.

Bartow further went on to say that he had taken a pledge to meet all the consequences of secession and felt honor bound to be among the first to meet any bloody circumstances. His cause was one of total commitment and he had boasted to fellow officers that he would only leave the field in victory regardless of the cost. Even his wife was informed that if necessary, he would prefer to die on the field of battle in defense of his country. There could be no doubt that Bartow was a firebrand.

The Oglethorpe Light Infantry didn't have long to wait for action to come to come their way. It was only two months after leaving Savannah and upon their arrival in Virginia that Bartow's troops were assigned to the Georgia Regiment of Volunteers. To no one's surprise, other independent units in the state had volunteered as well. They were united together to form the 8th Georgia Regiment. Bartow was promoted to Colonel and given the command of the 7th, 8th and 9th Georgia regiments. This command meant he was given a field promotion to brigadier general although he did not carry the actual commission.

A few weeks later Bartow was appointed commander of a brigade under Gen. Joseph E. Johnston. Gen. Thomas J. (Stonewall) Jackson commanded one of the other brigades, also under Johnston. Field commander Gen. Beauregard sent out an urgent request for reinforcements to his army of 23,000 who were facing a federal army of 35,000. By train and by foot, Bartow's brigade answered the call along with others and

Sherman Takes Savannah

arrived at Beauregard's position in somewhat a piecemeal fashion.

This came about since there weren't enough trains to accommodate Bartow's entire brigade so three of his five regiments remained behind. True to his cavalier form, Bartow himself took the first train and left the station riding in the coal tender behind the engine.

Bartow's unit was comprised of the youth of Savannah and was referred to as the BBB's, which stood for, Bartow's Beardless Boys. Although the unit thought of themselves as soldiers and men, most were unmarried and most were under twenty years of age. Still, they resented being looked on as children. Bartow, with his persuasive tongue, had secured for them the honor of being in the opening battle that was scheduled to begin early the next morning. He assured his men they would acquit themselves well but also admonished them to remember that wars and battles were serious stuff and that by sunset the following day, not all would be alive.

Bartow was eager to get into the fight and Beauregard assured him that his troops would be among the first deployed. Just after daybreak, Union forces tried to overrun the rebels' left flank. It was the South's weakest point and Confederate forces were in danger of being routed.

Jackson's brigade came up at that point as well as other reinforcements to bolster the disorganized rebel army. This was the action at Bull Run that would give Jackson the name of "Stonewall" that he immortalized. Gen. Barnard E. Bee of South Carolina, who commanded one of Johnston's other brigades, was preparing to lead an assault of desperation. He admonished his men to look at Jackson's brigade as they were standing like a "stone wall." It was Bee's last opportunity to burnish anything into history. He lay dying a few moments later.

Bartow was impetuous as usual and unable to wait so he rode off to find out what was going on. Not much time had

H. Ronald Freeman

elapsed before he returned at a full gallop and announced that they must go at once to the extreme left of the line so they couldn't be flanked by Union troops. The men set off at the double quick for five miles. They stopped in a cornfield planted on a small hill. Here the men received their baptism by fire when they were spotted by a Union battery that opened up on them.

Bartow's Brigade was blasted into a confused mess but some of the troops proved to be cool under fire and reassembled to march back toward the front. There they joined with the remnants of Bee's brigade and formed for battle to the left of Gen. Jackson's position.

Bartow sought out Beauregard and asked, "What shall I do, tell me, and if in the power of man, I will do it." Beauregard pointed to the left and forward. "Take that position," he said. He was ordered to rally the 7th Georgia troops under the immediate command of C. Locus J. Gartrell and position themselves on Jackson's right. Bartow rode back to the 7th and in true Bartow fashion grabbed the regimental flag and said, "Follow me and I will show you where."

Bartow rode off and in locating the assigned position admonished his men to hold it at all costs. Almost immediately a heavy barrage of Union artillery tore up their lines and was followed by mass of screaming Union troops. Bartow was riding among his boys still carrying the regimental banner when he was struck in the lower leg and knocked from the saddle to the ground. His horse was struck and killed by another random shot but he quickly found another mount.

He quickly was again astride and exhorted his men to attack and seize a Union battery. He rode among his men and told them to prepare to charge. He gave the regimental banner back to its rightful bearer and immediately was struck with a mortal wound near the heart. Bartow clutched his chest and began sliding from the saddle. He knew this was it. As he fell Col. Gartrell caught him and eased him to the ground. His

Sherman Takes Savannah

nearby officers and men came up around him and with shocked expression looked down on their leader.

Bartow knew there would be no second chance. The wound was fatal. With both hands clasped over his breast, he raised his head with a god-like effort, his eyes glittering in their last gleam with a far-away light. Bartow struggled to speak and finally said with gasping voice, "They have killed me boys, but don't you ever give up the field." He was carried from the field and died shortly thereafter.

His men didn't surrender the field but only held it at great cost. The Georgia 8th Regiment was in the thick of some of the heaviest fighting of the day. It suffered 207 wounded out of a total of 500.

The battle continued and by late afternoon the tide had shifted. Johnston's army received further reinforcements and the Union army was routed in a full-fledged retreat back toward Washington.

Being the first encounter of the war, it was a time when leaders were also present on the field. During the day, President Jefferson Davis arrived and visited the wounded in Confederate field hospitals. He was especially distressed to learn of the deaths of Bartow and Bee, both his personal friends. He asked that their bodies be placed on his special train and transported from the battlefield back to Richmond where they would lie in state for several days.

As always, with deaths in battle, the hardest part is informing the next of kin. Bartow's wife was also in Richmond, having traveled there so she could be near her husband. How would she be told? Jefferson Davis' wife Varina, offered to break the bad news to Mrs. Bartow, her personal friend. When she called on Mrs. Bartow any words were unnecessary, her pale face revealed the news before her voice had to. As soon as she walked into the room and Mrs. Bartow saw her face, she knew. She hid her face in her shawl and said, "Is it bad news for me? Is he killed?" Yes, it was bad news indeed of the worst kind.

Bartow's body was returned to Savannah a week after his death and was accompanied on the train by an escort from the Oglethorpe Light Infantry. He lay in state in the City Exchange for two days. From there he was placed in a black hearse drawn by four grays for the few blocks to Christ Church for the funeral. The streets were lined with weeping and silent onlookers. A column of troops made up from Savannah's military units was there to accompany the hearse. Bells tolled and cannon boomed as the procession moved through the town. All the military units in the city turned out and crowds thronged the streets in mourning as he passed.

After the funeral, the column moved slowly to Laurel Grove Cemetery where he was buried with military honors. The *Daily Morning News* said it was "the most solemn and imposing spectacle we have ever witnessed in Savannah." The city and the state had its first war hero and shortly thereafter Cass County was renamed as Bartow County in his honor.

It was not only Bartow that Savannah lost. The Oglethorpe's also lost six men killed who were childhood friends and even members of the same Sunday school class at Independent Presbyterian Church. They were buried on the battlefield at Bull Run but their remains were later returned to Savannah. One of them, Thomas Purse, Jr., was the son of Thomas Purse who would become Savannah's next mayor; His sister would later marry James Pierpont, the composer of *Jingle Bells.*

Sherman Takes Savannah

Fort Pulaski

Cockspur Island lies between the north and south channels of the Savannah River and about one mile from Tybee Island on the coast. It's a small tract of land over a mile long and about a half-mile wide. This island was the first place in the new world where John Wesley, founder of Methodism, set foot and preached his first sermon. Even in early days the Island had been the site of a fort guarding access to Savannah. In the Colonial period Ft. King George was erected and stood until its dismantling in 1776. It was replaced after the revolution in 1795 by Ft. Greene, named after Revolutionary War hero Nathanael Greene. That fortification was a six-gun earth and log battery enclosed by a palisade, but in 1804 a powerful hurricane struck the coast and removed all traces of it. Many in the garrison were drowned. Not too long after, plans were begun for a new fort - bigger, stronger and better.

During the War of 1812 with England, the United States realized how porous the coastal defenses were in that the British could and did come ashore wherever they chose. To remedy the situation, Congress appropriated funds for a system of coastal defenses. In Savannah, French Brigadier General Simon Bernard, was highly recommended for the job of constructing the new fort. He had served as chief military engineer to Napoleon and had come to the U.S. in 1815. He was selected but due to a delay in funding, the project was not begun until 1829.

Work finally commenced but was halted each summer because of the danger posed by malaria, typhoid, dysentery, and yellow fever. Workers were brought back to the site in the fall. Progress was also delayed by hurricanes, freezing winds, and occasional lack of funding. Skilled workers were recruited from across the United States and slaves were hired from nearby rice plantations to supply additional labor. This was not an uncommon practice at the time where slave

Sherman Takes Savannah

holders could rent out their workers and earn additional income.

Young Robert E. Lee, a second lieutenant with a degree in engineering from West Point, was dispatched to Cockspur Island. It was 1829 and he was on his first assignment. His orders were to assist in the completion of the fort. Lee served at Pulaski for 17 months.

In 1847, after eighteen years of exhausting work, Ft. Pulaski was completed at a cost of one million dollars. It was considered state-of-the-art at the time having five sides, two to guard the south channel of the river, two to guard the north channel and one facing west. The fort's perimeter had a circumference of 1,580 feet and the enclosed parade ground was two and one-half acres in size. The walls were seven to nine feet thick and rose twenty-five feet above a moat forty-eight feet wide and seven feet deep. Although it was intended that the fort be armed with 146 cannon, half on top of the fort and the remainder in brick casemates below, Pulaski received only 20 long 32-pounder naval guns.

The fort was designed to be impregnable. Twenty-five million bricks and eighteen years had gone into its construction. he bricks for the walls were manufactured at Hermitage Plantation west of Savannah. The bricks for the embrasures and interior walls that needed to be harder were shipped from

Fort Pulaski

Sherman Takes Savannah

Virginia and Maryland. The finishing trim was made of New York granite and Connecticut River valley sandstone.

The only choices for coastal defense in the early nineteenth century were large fleets positioned at each harbor or strategically located forts. Obviously a fleet would be expensive and need constant repair and extensive manpower. A fort was far more economical but its design had to accomplish its two main purposes: preventing the passage of ships and to resisting land attack. To resist attack from the land, a fort had to be inaccessible. Pulaski fulfilled this requirement very well.

Thirty years after his first assignment, Lee returned to the fort. It was then 1861 and he was a general in the Confederate Army. His new assignment was to inspect and strengthen coastal defenses.

Lee expressed in a letter to his daughter that he was concerned about defenses along the coast based on the small number of men and arms he was able to muster. It was surprising to him the large number of men the North had thrown thus far at blockading the South.

Lee knew eventually Union batteries would be placed on Tybee Island and from there the Union gunners would attempt to breach Pulaski's thick walls. He tried to assuage the concerns of the officers commanding the fort. "They will make it pretty hot for you but they can't breach your walls from that distance," said Lee.

Union Captain Quincey A. Gillmore thought otherwise. He had been sent from Hilton Head to Tybee Island to determine whether or not it would be feasible to attempt the destruction of the fort from that distance. Gillmore, after observing, reported back to his superiors, "I deem the reduction of that work practicable by batteries of mortars and rifled guns established on Tybee Island."

However, his superiors were more in agreement with Lee. The Chief Engineer of the army, General Joseph Totem, said the fort could not be taken with any number of guns of manageable calibers in a month's firing. As for the use of rifled cannon, they believed their effective use had not yet been proven. Most experts agreed that heavy artillery was ineffective at ranges over 800 yards. Tybee to Pulaski was more than twice that distance at its nearest point.

President Davis suddenly recalled Lee to Richmond naming as his replacement Gen. John C. Pemberton of Pennsylvania as the commander of Confederate coastal forces. Pemberton established his headquarters at Charleston and focused on continuing Lee's work in strengthening Savannah and Charleston. Although a northerner, Pemberton had married a southern girl and had made strong friendships with his southern classmates at West Point so his alliance with the South was not surprising.

Quincey A. Gillmore

Union generals decided to go ahead with the assault on Pulaski even though most thought at best they would only shake the walls of the fort. Command of Union forces in the area was passed to Gen. David Hunter, who continued with the gun emplacements on Tybee. Hunter had family connections in Savannah being an uncle of Eleanor Kinzie Gordon whose husband was a Confederate officer. Their daughter was Juliette who in later years as Juliette Gordon Low would establish the Girl Scouts of America.

Sherman Takes Savannah

Union batteries were placed at ranges from 1,650 to 3,400 yards. Locating the guns on Tybee Island was an engineering marvel in itself. Most of the work was done under cover of darkness so the Confederates would not be able to zero in on Union positions. Hidden by a ridge of sand, men labored many nights to prepare the gun emplacements. As difficult as it was, only at its completion did the real work begin.

The mortars weighing up to eight and a half tons each had to be unloaded from ships to barges and then towed ashore by rowboats through the surf at high tide. When the tide went out the guns were hauled to higher ground. From there they had to be rolled and dragged over a distance of two miles through mud, marsh, sand and sawgrass.

To move even one of the huge 17,000-pound guns took the efforts of 250 men with ample rope and carts. When the carts sank into the mire, the gun would have to be unloaded and rolled over planks to solid ground where it would await

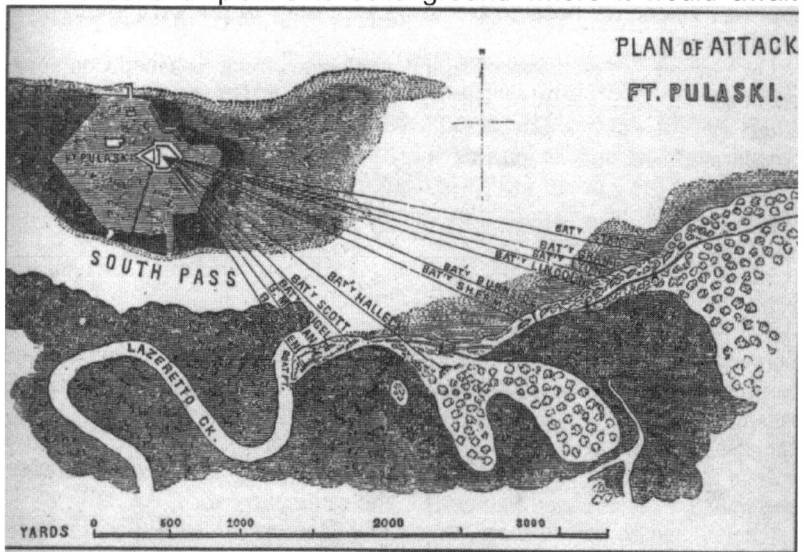

reloading to the cart after it was unstuck from the mud. It could take hundreds of men hours merely to move the guns less than

H. Ronald Freeman

a hundred yards. Once on high ground the guns had to be moved to the battery sites that could be hundreds of yards away.

Through great exertion, and with considerable accident and injury, they dragged 16 mortars, 10 regular cannon and 10 rifled guns into a line of batteries that were located along a mile and a half stretch running from the northwest point of Tybee Island along Lazaretto Creek facing in the direction of Ft. Pulaski. The guns were supplied with 900 rounds apiece and a store of 9,600 pounds of gunpowder was stockpiled near Tybee Light. Their intention was to level the fort if it did not surrender.

As the federals worked at night, they were besieged by swarms of sand gnats and mosquitoes. Bitten but undeterred, by April 9, 1862, they were ready. Orders were issued to each of the guns relative to the rate of fire, charges and elevation. The Rebels could see the changes in the sand dunes and sensed the attack was about to begin.

On the Confederate side within the fort, sand was spread around the guns and many of the men wrote farewell letters and even last will and testaments. The garrison surgeon sharpened his knives and saws. Logistically, setting up the guns was yeoman's work. The fort had already been isolated from the mainland by having its telegraph line cut and two Union batteries upstream had made supplying the fort impossible.

Pulaski was now hemmed in from all sides. Only an occasional messenger was able to slip to and from Savannah. The garrison realized more and more that reinforcements would not be forthcoming. They also knew that Georgia's "Mosquito Fleet" would be no match for the Yankee gunboats so they could expect no help from that source either.

Sherman Takes Savannah

Pulaski was being defended by 385 Confederate troops behind numerous large guns and seven and a half foot walls. Commanding was 24-year-old Col. Charles H. Olmstead. Although some thought he didn't have the "right stuff" for command, he was intelligent and possessed a great deal of common sense. He was popular and had been elected colonel by his men. His initial charge was to carry out Lee's recommendations concerning strengthening the defenses of the fort.

If the Union soldiers were hard at work getting their guns into place, the southern troops worked just as hard in readying their defenses. Heavy timbers were placed around the interior perimeter to protect the casements from shell fragments. Ditches were dug to catch rolling shells and unused embrasures were walled up. From the ramparts of Pulaski, the defenders could see from 60 to 70 Union vessels along the coast.

Charles Olmstead

On April 9, 1862, after intensive months of preparation, there was a last minute rush by Union troops to make ready. All the men were busy until late hours in the evening. Both sides knew, through reconnoitering and general feeling that the hour was at hand. At 5:30 a.m. the following morning, Union Lt. James Wilson under a flag of truce carried a message to the commanding officer at Ft. Pulaski.

H. Ronald Freeman

Soldiers in the fort observed the approaching vessel as it crossed the south channel and had little doubt of its mission. That morning when the garrison at Pulaski awoke and looked across to Tybee they could see the sand dunes in front of the guns had been leveled and now the guns looked directly at them with menacing barrels.

Maj. Gen. David Hunter, now in command of Union forces outside Pulaski, signed the surrender demand that Wilson carried. Hunter's demand in a matter-of-fact manner specified the number of his guns, their caliber and their point of readiness. He stated there would be no doubt as to the outcome of the bombardment. Since he wished to avoid a useless waste of life he allowed 30 minutes for Pulaski's commander to respond.

"I can only say that I am here to defend the fort, not to

Fort Pulaski Under Attack

Sherman Takes Savannah

surrender it," replied Col. Olmstead. Upon receiving the reply, Gen. Hunter told Gillmore, who had been brevetted a brigadier general, to commence firing as soon as he pleased. The first of 5,275 shells was fired at 7:40 a.m.

By 8:15 the Union barrage began for real and by 9:30 all Union batteries were participating in the fray. The Rebels returned fire but they were firing blind since the Yankee batteries were still somewhat concealed. The guns of Ft. Pulaski that bore on Tybee Island quickly and energetically fired but with little effect. The Federal batteries were shielded by ridge and by sandbags and Confederate shot fell in front of and behind the guns. By 1:00 p.m. the afternoon the new rifled Federal cannon had smashed gaping indentures in Pulaski's walls.

Confederate Gen. Pemberton was not concerned that the fort was under attack. In fact he had returned to his headquarters in Charleston. In his opinion Pulaski was impregnable and it would be a waste of ammunition to even bother to return fire. What he didn't know was that the Union guns were close to implementing a breach in the walls that would expose the fort's interior to further bombardment and attack.

John Pemberton

As predicted by most military minds, the Union mortar fire and the Columbiad smooth-bores were ineffective. Not so with the new rifled cannon. From them, the shells drilled into the walls like

H. Ronald Freeman

bits from an auger. Seeing their effectiveness, the shelling was concentrated on one spot on the wall that soon gave off a very blotchy appearance. Return fire from the fort was sporadic and did little harm. The Union guns were firing about seven shells per minute or about 400 to the hour.

Near sunset there was the beginning of a small hole through the masonry of the wall where the Union firing had been concentrated. After sundown the shelling ceased except a few periodic shots throughout the evening to prevent the rebels from repairing the fort. Olmstead took the opportunity of the pause to inspect the damage. He was not prepared for what he found. Three of his casements in the wall had been exposed by the rifled shot. Pulaski's ability to respond to the enemy guns had been severely diminished. The fort was left with only half of its original twenty guns that had pointed in the direction of the enemy on Tybee Island.

At the crack of dawn the enemy guns were at it again.

Damage to Pulaski

Sherman Takes Savannah

Preparations were being made for an infantry assault as well. It was felt the breach in the walls would be widened to the extent that it would be difficult for the rebels to defend. The moat was soon filled with so much masonry from the wall that soldiers could walk across without wetting their feet.

By noon two casements on the southeast wall had been blown open and shells were flying through to the parade ground and approaching the magazine on the opposing wall. The magazine held over 40,000 pounds of black powder and had already suffered the loss of one of its walls.

By 1:30 in the afternoon, three casements had been breached and shot was pouring through at will. Now the powder magazine of the fort was in the direct line of fire. Although the gunners inside were gallant, their guns were ineffectual and as a result none of the Union guns were damaged and only one Union soldier had been killed.

By 2:00 p.m. three shells had struck just outside the magazine and scattered the ordnance squad in panic. The defenders were now in desperate straits. There were no reinforcements coming and their means to resist had been diminished indeed. Col. Olmstead called his officers together for a conference. All knew that one well-placed shell could destroy the magazine and the subsequent explosion would kill most of the men in the fort. They agreed unanimously that the risk was too great and that surrender was the only option. Otherwise, the garrison would face certain destruction. A cease-fire was ordered and Col. Olmstead fixed a white sheet to a rammer and lowered the flag.

The battle was over. What took 18 years and 25 million bricks to build had been shelled into submission in a mere 32 hours. Olmstead defended his decision by knowing it was only a matter of time before the magazine would explode at great loss of life.

H. Ronald Freeman

Gen. Hunter, in command of the U.S. Department of the South, was not an active participant in the battle. By the time his assistant adjutant-general, Maj. Charles G. Halpine arrived, it was late afternoon. This would be the formal surrender. The victors set out across the channel to receive the surrender but choppy waters delayed their crossing. It was almost comical. Here was a fort waiting to surrender and the conquerors were unable to move in and take possession of what they had won.

Olmstead met Gillmore's party personally and he asked that only Gillmore enter the fort to hammer out the terms of surrender. The request was honored and the two met for about an hour to negotiate the terms of the agreement.

The surrender proceedings were held in Col. Olmstead's quarters. By this time it was dusk and only the light of candles illuminated the interior. Everyone stood. All of the garrison's officers, in the sequence of their rank, laid their swords on the table and made a statement. Olmstead was last and said, "I yield my sword, but I trust I have not disgraced it."

Other captured officers of the garrison spoke as defiantly as ever. Gen. Gillmore took his leave and Maj. Halpine assumed command of the surrender negotiations. He was generous and responded that, "it is a painful duty to receive the swords of men who have shown by their bravery that they deserve to wear them." Afterward, Olmstead gave his captors a tour of the fort while the Yankees and rebels mingled exchanging jeers and jests.

At the close of the ceremony, the Union officers withdrew to give Olmstead the courtesy of speaking some final words to his officers. The U.S. flag was raised over the fort and it was now in Union hands again.

A few realized the military importance of what had happened, not only in the current conflict but also on the wider field of military strategy. The whole system of warfare had been revolutionized. Brick was no longer any better than butter as a means to resist modern weapons utilizing rifled cannon. It was the beginning of the end in the use of static fortifications to

Sherman Takes Savannah

guard positions and withstand the enemy. Much the same way as the engagement of the ironclads Monitor and Merrimac had changed naval warfare; Ft. Pulaski would change the tactics on land.

None of the federal guns sustained damage whereas they had silenced 16 of the 20 Confederate guns the fort trained on Tybee. The Yankees only suffered one casualty and that was a young private mortally wounded by an exploding shell in one of the batteries. The southerners suffered one killed and twelve wounded.

The Union gunners used 5,275 shells, only a fifth of their total supply of ammunition. They had been prepared for a week of siege. Both sides realized the significance of the new rifled guns in warfare and knew it was a revolution in traditional military strategy.

Although Gen. Gillmore agreed with Olmstead's request to allow the southern sick and wounded to be transported back to Confederate lines, Hunter refused. These men were sent along with the others to prisons in the New York harbor.

Some disagreed with Olmstead's surrender thinking he shouldn't have turned over a fort with a well-supplied magazine regardless of how damaged the fort may have been. Some felt he lacked nerve and should have died a hero rather than having his reputation open to question. Olmstead, even in later years, adhered to his decision being proper since there was nothing else that could have been done.

Rifled Cannon

In 1841, Rhode Island militia general Charles T. James developed the smoothbore gun rifled with a series of lands and grooves. The lower half of the shell was encased in a greased canvas jacket. When the gun was fired expanding gases forced the soft lead into the grooves that the greased canvas served to lubricate.

H. Ronald Freeman

When a barrel is rifled with lands and grooves, the discharge explosion drives the soft material at the base of the projectile into the grooves and forces it to take the rifling that imparts the spin necessary to keep the shell oriented during its flight toward its path. The problem with the muzzle loading of rifled artillery was that the shell must be able to be inserted easily down the barrel even when it's partially fouled with residue and yet take the rifling when the charge ignites and the shell is discharged. Rifled shells used less than a quarter of the charge needed by their smoothbore cousins since no gas escaped around the shell itself. It was also important that the projectile was seated on the powder charge. If space existed between the powder and the projectile the blast would not cause the soft part of the shell to engage the grooves. The shell would fall after leaving the gun and fall inaccurately short. The penetration of a masonry wall by a rifled shell was greater than that of a ball of equal weight since the shell presented less area for wind resistance and had greater final velocity.

The rifled shells penetrated twice the depth of the solid round shot and penetrated at least 18 inches before exploding. One problem with the rifled James guns was that the rifling fouled easily with powder residue even though the gun crew kept the tube clean with a special scraper. Although the shells came wrapped in greased canvas and were again greased just before firing, fouling was a problem. The accuracy of the James guns was a direct result of keeping the rifling clean with the scraper. This was attached to the end of the rammer head and consisted of several strips of steel equal to the number of grooves in the barrel. Using the scraper after every five or six firings enabled smooth performance of the James guns. Although James himself developed a scraper to clean the rifle grooves, it was not present with the gun's supplies and Gillmore had to improvise.

The rifled guns accounted for almost sixty percent of the breaching damage to the fort. Had Gillmore known how effective they would be he could have shortened the eight

Sherman Takes Savannah

laborious weeks of preparation to only one week. He could have eliminated the heavy mortars, the Columbiads and the long distance batteries.

H. Ronald Freeman

Bracing for Attack

With Pulaski's surrender, the city was in a constant fear of attack. The work being done by local residents in obstructing passage up the Savannah River increased. Large ballast stones from the ramps on River Street were sunk in wooden cribs in the north and south channels below Ft. Jackson. Sixteen vessels were also sunk nearby. In the same area, the floating battery *Georgia* was moored near the obstructions. This was primarily because the *Georgia* was so unseaworthy that her only use was as a fail-safe battery in the event Union ships were able to penetrate that far upriver.

The Union blockade had been a menace up to that point but not a threat. Establishing a defense would require the transferring of thousands of men to the coast that otherwise could have been deployed in the front lines of the Confederate armies.

Savannah, more than any other city in the South, was said to be instilled with a military air. Men everywhere were in uniform and the uniforms were as varied as colors in the rainbow. Some red, some white, some with coats and some without. Even the caps were different.

The only thing the men who converged on Savannah in military units seemed to be in accord on was that the insects had to be worse than the enemy. Heading the list were mosquitoes followed by fleas and sandgnats.

After the fall of Ft. Pulaski, many expected the Union army to march on in to Savannah. It didn't happen. The federals were reticent to move because they didn't have sufficient knowledge about rebel activity in the town. They didn't know the strength of the city's naval force or how many forts upriver defended the city. Lacking this information, they were content to just hold Pulaski.

Upriver from Pulaski the rebels had two primary forts; Jackson and Bartow. Jackson had been erected during the war of 1812 and Bartow, built in 1861 and named for the fallen

Sherman Takes Savannah

hero, was an earthen fort at the junction of the Savannah and Wilmington Rivers erected on seventeen acres at Causton Bluff. This was about ten miles upriver from Pulaski. The idea was that the Yankees would have to run the gauntlet if they decided to proceed from the sea to Savannah. The headquarters for river defense, including that of the navy, would be at Ft. Jackson. It was commanded by Col. Edward Anderson of Savannah. Across the river from Jackson, two other batteries were built so they could effect a crossfire. These were named Cheves and Lawton.

Two days after Pulaski's surrender, Gen. Hunter, who was a strong abolitionist, issued an order abolishing all slaveholdings on the island where Pulaski was located. Then, he decreed the slaves in the entire states of Georgia, Florida and South Carolina were free from their former masters. Abolitionists cheered but Hunter's officers and men opposed the edict. They were not in the fight to put an end to slavery but to preserve the Union. President Lincoln moved quickly to revoke the action thinking the timing was premature for such extremism so early in the war.

Gen. David Hunter

Another landmark decision was reached shortly after Pulaski fell. This time it was on the Confederate side. Their congress passed the Conscription Act stating every young man between the ages of 18 and 35 would be required to serve in the military for three years or until the war ended. This meant that the Georgia militia would become Confederate troops and fight for the South. This didn't sit well with the men. Many had

H. Ronald Freeman

enlisted to fight for states' rights and the new law was quite unpopular.

In October 1862, Gen. John Pemberton was transferred to department command in Mississippi and eastern Louisiana and promoted to lieutenant general. His replacement was the little Cajun general Pierre G. T. Beauregard who had led the assault on Ft. Sumter in Charleston but had not distinguished himself since the first battle of Bull Run. He, like Pemberton, made his headquarters in Charleston where they were convinced the Union offensive would be directed.

Beauregard was an 1838 graduate of West Point and a native of Louisiana. He had served with Robert E. Lee on Gen. Winfield Scott's staff in the Mexican War. In 1861, he was appointed superintendent of West Point but because of his pro-southern sentiments was relieved almost immediately. Subsequently he resigned his commission and was awarded a Confederate brigadier general's commission soon after entering the southern army.

Sherman Takes Savannah

Ft. McAllister

The fort had been named for Col. George Washington McAllister whose son owned the land donated for the construction of a fort. Whereas Ft. Pulaski was guarding Savannah's front door, Ft. McAllister was guarding the rear.

It provided protection for the Gulf Railroad bridge as well. Union naval officers described the fort as being crammed with bomb proofs and traverses so much as to look as though the spaces were actually carved from the earth.

Fort McAllister

In 1862 McAllister had several encounters with Federal gunboats where neither the fort nor the boats gained an advantage or did any serious damage to one another. In January the following year, the fort was to again be tested, this time against the new federal ironclads.

The strategic plan was for five of the new ironclads to enter the port of Charleston and demand its surrender. Once successful there, the boats would then attack Savannah. But first, they needed a trial run. Ft. McAllister was chosen as the proving ground. Enter the *Montauk,* a 200-foot state-of-the-art monitor type boat. It boasted a revolving turret with two Dahlgren cannons, one an eleven inch and the other a fifteen.

Her mission was to destroy the fort and to burn the railroad trestle stretching over the Ogeechee River. The question was finally on the table. Were ironclads the equal of forts? Here at McAllister, they hoped to find a positive answer.

Commander of the fort was Maj. John B. Gallie of Savannah with troop support from Col. Robert H. Anderson. Gallie was a 56-year-old Scotsman and a former captain in the Chatham Artillery.

On January 27, 1863, after reconnoitering the rebel obstructions in small boats, the *Montauk,* led a five-ship flotilla up the Ogeechee to within 1500 yards of McAllister. Her captain was John Worden, who had commanded the ironclad *Monitor* as she fought the *Merrimac* in March 1862 in the classic battle in Hampton Roads, Virginia. During that battle he was inflicted with a temporary blindness from a shell exploding on the pilothouse. This injury forced him to relinquish his command during the battle but Congress voted a show of thanks not once but twice in recognizing his heroism and

Sherman Takes Savannah

leadership. He was promoted from lieutenant to commander and given command of the *Montauk* in December 1862. She was a sister ship of the *Monitor*.

He was eager to try her new Dahlgren guns against the fort's earthen walls. As the shelling commenced, the *Montauk* and her sister gunboats fired over three hundred shells at the fort. The *Montauk* even hurled sixty-one fifteen-inch cannon shot, the largest yet made, at the fort over a span of five hours. Gaping holes were torn in the earth each time they fired. Sod and sand flew in all directions. That was pretty much the extent of it. The *Montauk* did little damage to McAllister's sand and mud batteries. The shells dug huge craters in McAllister's walls, but that night the damage was filled in with sand. The Confederates suffered no casualties.

John L. Worden

On the other side, the fort gave as well as it got. It scored fifteen hits on the ironclad. The result was a disappointing fifteen small dents. A northern journalist described the effect as being much the same as throwing beans against a brick wall.

H. Ronald Freeman

The only logical halt to the battle was a diminishing supply of ammunition on the part of the ironclads. Having expended all, the boats withdrew. Each side called it a victory. The South reported the attack had been repulsed and no one was injured. On the northern side they had demonstrated the ability of an ironclad to withstand shore batteries. The earthen fort still remained and only needed a little grooming where craters existed from the bombardment.

Undeterred, the Union gunboats came back for another try, this time in February. The result was pretty much the same. The *Montauk* was hit 48 times but with little effect. On the southern side, again very little damage was sustained to the fort but a major loss was suffered on the human side. Maj. John Gallie, the Savannahian who commanded McAllister, received his fatal wound when the cannon where he was standing took a hit and either a shell fragment or shrapnel took off the top of his head. He had suffered a minor wound to the face earlier but refused to leave his post. The fort again proved its resiliency and by morning the major craters were covered and on the whole it was again in a defensible position.

Unknown to the federals during this attack, trapped upriver in the Ogeechee was the rebel blockade-runner *Nashville (*re-commissioned as the *CSS Rattlesnake)*. She had been in the river since July 1862 when she slipped in from England, laden with military supplies. Her holds were unloaded into smaller boats and transported to the Atlantic & Gulf Railroad bridge where the cargo was carried by train into Savannah.

She was a 1200-ton side-wheeler built in 1853. She had been extremely successful in eluding the Union navy and attacking their shipping on open seas. Prior to the war, she had been in passenger service but was seized at Charleston in 1861, impressed into Confederate service and converted into a blockade-runner.

Sherman Takes Savannah

The *Nashville* had been unable to find an opening in the

C.S.S. Nashville under Fire

offshore Yankee blockade and had been forced to head back upriver in the Ogeechee. She was unfortunate and ran aground on a sandbar near the fort. Even with the aid of a tug, the rebels were unable to dislodge the steamer. The Union ironclad quickly spotted the blockade-runner's predicament and planned for an attack the following morning.

The *Montauk* and two gunboats started upriver at 4:00 a.m. on February 28th and verified the *Nashville* was hopelessly grounded. The gunboats attempted to engage McAllister's guns, while the fort fired at all three vessels. McAllister's cannons tried frantically to protect the *Nashville* and blasted the *Montauk* with all available guns but to no avail. It was all in vain.

The *Montauk* opened fire on the *Nashville* from 1,200 yards and immediately the boat was in flames. The crew was forced to abandon ship and witnessed the explosion of the magazine and the ship. Although only the masts and stacks of

H. Ronald Freeman

the raider were visible, the *Montauk's* fifth shot plowed into the *Nashville's* hull. Three additional shells followed in rapid succession. After the firing paused to let the smoke settle, the northern newspaper correspondent on location wrote, "We saw to our great joy a dense column of smoke rising from the forward deck of the stranded vessel. Our exploding shell had set her on fire. A few minutes more, and flames were distinctly visible, forcing their way up, gradually creeping aft until they had reached nearly to the base of the smokestack."

The *Nashville's* crew had abandoned ship when the ironclad started firing, and they watched helplessly from a distance as the fire spread to her magazine. At 9:45 a.m. the ship's ammunition was set off with a roar that reportedly rattled windows in Savannah.

To the Confederates satisfaction, the *Montauk* also hit a bit of bad luck after the shelling. Throughout this action, the Rebels had been frustrated by the failure of their torpedoes to destroy a federal vessel. Many of the mines were defective, while the powder in some had become sodden and Union work parties had removed others under the veil of darkness. As the *Montauk* proceeded

Sherman Takes Savannah

downriver in stately fashion toward the sound, she hit a torpedo that did explode. The *Montauk's* engineer described it as "a violent, sudden, and seemingly double explosion." He dashed about the ship trying to determine whether the ironclad had been bored by a cannon shot or if a boiler had exploded.

The pilot had ignored a feeling of danger moments earlier by plowing over a piece of cloth, which apparently marked the location of the torpedo for the Confederates. Her hull was torn with a gaping 10-foot rip in her side that forced her to run aground for repairs. The pilot quickly beached the *Montauk* on a sandbar. That maneuver gave the crew time to cover the hole in her hull with mud and temporarily stem the leak. Even her pumps couldn't keep her afloat and a replacement section of the boiler had to be used as a temporary patch. She was towed back to Port Royal for repairs.

The North demonstrated their tenaciousness and mounted a flotilla in March to try again to take McAllister. The earthen fortification still mocked the ironclads. The northern raiding party this time was comprised of three ironclads, three gunboats and three motor schooners. The gunboats were the *Passaic,* the *Nahant* and the *Patapsco.* The Union commanders felt the outing would be little more than a day's target practice at Ft. McAllister.

The *Passaic* was struck 34 times, and like her sister boats earlier, with small effect. On land, McAllister was fired at 224 times with not more than 50 shells finding their target. After seven hours, the only casualties were Capt. Drayton of the *Passaic* who received slight facial wounds from deck fragments and the pet tomcat of the fort that was struck and killed. The ironclads decided the small earthen fort not to be worth further effort on their part and headed off toward Charleston. The lesson learned by the Confederates was that ironclads no longer held any terror for them.

H. Ronald Freeman

An obvious question also arises of why didn't the Confederate Navy in Savannah come to the aid of McAllister? As odd as it seems, there was no passage by water that allowed the Confederates to reach Ossabaw Sound and enter the Ogeechee River that was not impeded by obstacles in the water or guarded by the Union gunboats blockading the coast.

Sherman Takes Savannah

Town Without Pity

The war seemed to grind on and with the southern defeats at Vicksburg and Gettysburg, the gloom in the spring of 1863 was pervasive. The South was becoming tired and despondent. Any thinking person could see what was happening and yet could not accept it. From the drumbeat and frenzy of war in 1861 the South was now shocked into a realism from which there was no escape. There was a great weariness of war and a desire to go home among most of the men. The Confederacy was withering but the idea of giving up was so negative that most southerners could not reconcile themselves to it.

Many in the South looked for divine intervention. Something would happen. It had to. They couldn't give up hope. They knew God was on their side and knowing that, of what could they fear? They knew they must suffer but also that their cause was God's cause and they would be delivered. It would just be in God's time and not in theirs.

The dilemma that led to despair was now defined. The South may not have known which road to take but it knew that there was one option that would never be palatable. Reunion with the North was just not acceptable. Reconstruction was impossible - unthinkable. It was impossible to face. Only when the last brave soldier of the South had fallen, only then think of submission and capitulation.

As was usual, everyone looked for a scapegoat to blame. Many pointed to the president, Jefferson Davis. Not that he had done anything wrong, but only that he was the visible head and that all responsibility for improper action, or inaction, should rest with him.

Others, including Gazaway B. Lamar, the Confederate financier, blamed the Confederate Congress. According to him, they had initiated a gigantic war solely on credit and had then taxed their people partially and unequally.

H. Ronald Freeman

Regardless of the party to blame, everyone knew that war was hanging above their heads and Gen. William Tecumseh Sherman was making himself and his army known on the battlefields of Chattanooga. Everyone felt the impending doom hanging over the South and especially in the state of Georgia.

Lt. Gen. William J. Hardee assumed command of the Department of South Carolina, Georgia and Florida. It was October 5, 1864 and he was 49 years old; a handsome officer with a military bearing, long hair and a well-trimmed mustache and goatee. He was a veteran from most of the western campaigns and considered to be one of the South's most able generals. He carried the nickname of "Old Reliable" by his men. He was a West Point graduate in the class of 1838.

Hardee had served as the commandant of cadets at West Point for four years from 1856 to 1860. He authored a military manual entitled *Rifle and Light Infantry Tactics* which was a guidebook to both sides during the war. When Georgia seceded, Hardee resigned his commission, accepted one in the Confederacy and soon rose to the rank of major general.

He was so well respected that he was offered the command of the Army of Tennessee when Gen. Braxton Bragg was relieved in the winter of 1863. He only accepted on an interim basis and refused the command that ultimately went to Joseph Johnston.

What did make Hardee somewhat miffed was when Gen. Hood, his junior in rank, was chosen over him to replace Johnston in the Atlanta campaign in July 1864. He felt Hood lacked the experience and ability necessary for so important a command. That was not the end of it. Hood blamed Hardee for not following through with an assault at Peachtree Creek. He attributed the failure directly to actions by Hardee. Later actions and tactics by Hood at Franklin and Nashville seemed to bear out Hardee's opinion.

The two were at loggerheads with Hood calling for Hardee to be relieved and Hardee requesting reassignment.

Sherman Takes Savannah

President Davis intervened and ordered Hardee to the South Atlantic command in October. Here, joined by Gen. Beauregard, he set about to bolster the defenses of Savannah and Charleston with the meager ten thousand troops allotted him.

H. Ronald Freeman

Sherman

Following his success in the western campaigns, Gen. Ulysses S. Grant had been promoted to Lieutenant General and Commander of all U.S. forces. It was March 1864. Succeeding him as Commander of the Military Division of the Mississippi was Maj. Gen. William T. Sherman who at that time was 44 years old. At that point in the war it was Sherman's charge to organize an invasion of Georgia. It would coincide with Grant's overwhelming army of men and materials that was pursuing Lee's retreating army from the north into Virginia. The two juggernauts would hopefully crush the Confederacy. But who was this Sherman? Where did he come from and what were his ideas?

Born in Lancaster, Ohio on February 8, 1820, he was one of eleven children and the sixth child and third son of Charles Sherman, an Ohio State Supreme Court justice. He was named Tecumseh after the powerful Indian chieftain who had been killed in the War of 1812. The chief had been admired as well as feared by the white settlers of the Great Lakes region. Charles Sherman died suddenly when little Tecumseh was nine. For financial reasons this forced his children to be taken in by friends and relatives.

Young Tecumseh was placed in the home of Senator Thomas Ewing, whose daughter would later become his wife. The Ewings lived only two houses up the street from the Shermans. The Ewings never formally adopted the boy primarily out of consideration for his mother. The story goes that the senator told Sherman's mother that he wanted one of the boys. He said, "Give me the brightest of the lot and I will make a man out of him." "Take Cump," his mother said, "he's the smartest."

Soon after Sherman entered the Ewing household, he was baptized in the Catholic Church and given what was felt to be a proper Christian first name. Since young Sherman was baptized on June 25th, St. William's Day, the priest chose the

Sherman Takes Savannah

name William for him. In spite of this, his boyhood moniker of "Cump" seemed to stick.

Through the senator's influence he was able to gain an appointment to West Point in 1836 where he stayed the course and graduated sixth in the class of 1840. While there, he did not excel as a cadet. Sherman was not considered a good soldier and was not selected for any cadet rank. He remained a private throughout his entire four years. The qualifications for rank were neatness in dress and a strict conformity to the rules. Sherman readily admitted to not excelling in either of those. He was among the best students but his demerits reduced his class standing from fourth to sixth.

Like most young West Point graduates of the time, Sherman saw action in the Mexican War. After thirteen years in the service he resigned his commission to become a bank executive in San Francisco. The man had such high integrity, especially in money matters, that there was never the slightest suspicion of wrongdoing about him.

An illustration of his integrity was when he was handling money for eastern friends and classmates seeking favorable investment on the Pacific coast. Gen. William Hardee and Gen. Braxton Bragg, later adversaries, were included in this group. Instead of treating these funds like any other bank deposits, he established a trust fund, placed the monies in promising investments and kept detailed records of dividends, profits, and interest. Much of these investments were in San Francisco municipal bonds when suddenly the financial panic of 1857 struck. As a result, the city declared bankruptcy and the investments became worthless.

Although Sherman had no legal obligation for the losses the investors had suffered, he felt personally responsible. His natural father had bankrupted his family and ruined his health by trying to repay self-imposed obligations long ago, rendering Sherman a dependent foster child as a result. Now he found himself in the same predicament but even more frightening since it involved his army family.

His friends had invested $136 thousand in 1847 dollars and about $20 thousand of that was lost. Those funds in 2006 dollars would be about $433,000. To make good on the investments, he was forced to sell 2,680 acres of California land as well as 640 acres in Illinois. Actually, he liquidated everything he owned and also borrowed money from his father-in-law, Senator Ewing. With proceeds from sales and borrowings in hand, Sherman refunded the original investment. The investors readily accepted although they had full knowledge that Sherman was suffering the loss.

Sherman as a Young Man

Because of the panic, the bank fell on hard times and Sherman entered the practice of law with his two stepbrothers in Leavenworth, Kansas. This, like other vocations, seemed to be an interim step and in 1859 he accepted the position of president of the college that would ultimately become Louisiana State University (L.S.U.). His friend and later adversary Braxton Bragg had highly recommended him. This position was vacated in January 1861 as the nation moved closer to war.

For five months, he headed a streetcar company in St. Louis but with the outbreak of war, he accepted the appointment of colonel of the 13th U.S. Infantry. It was in that post that he led his troops in the first battle of Bull Run and acquitted himself well. Afterwards, he was promoted to

Sherman Takes Savannah

brigadier general. A few months later he was ordered to join Gen. Henry W. Halleck in St. Louis. There he was given command of a division that had the misfortune to be overrun in the first day of fighting at Shiloh.

In May 1862, he was promoted to major general and participated in the federal campaign to open the Mississippi River. At Vicksburg, he was in command of the 15th Corps and was a key player in the battles around Chattanooga.

His customary manner was to walk along the road during his marches with his hands in his pockets and talk good common sense with the person nearest him regardless of rank. Sherman's slovenliness added to his casual allure since he knew his real merit rested in his authority and strength and not in some hollow and aloof spit and polish protocol. He was their "Uncle Billy," the all knowing but plain leader who shared their hardships while guiding them toward victory.

Sandy-headed and gaunt, with a grizzled short-cropped beard, Sherman had that "wild expression in his eyes" like Lazarus being raised from the dead. He was always drumming his slender fingers on a table or fiddling with his beard or fidgeting with the buttons on his coat. Anything to be active.

Sherman was a shade below six feet in height with a wiry muscular body. Although only in his forties, his face was etched with deep furrows. Then too, it was strange how they seemed to disappear when he

Gen. Sherman

H. Ronald Freeman

engaged children and women in conversation. His eyes were dark brown and intense. He also sported a prominent red nose, coarse red hands, and small bright eyes with a black felt hat slouched over them. His rebelliousness against tradition and authority was innate. However it was accompanied by a profound respect for law and order. He could be cool and logical but would temper it with compassion. He spoke in a colorful manner and sprinkled his descriptions with picturesque phrases. The man possessed an insatiable curiosity combined with a mental quickness and an acuteness of observation.

His ability to fall asleep was almost childlike. Whether the ground was wet or the floor hard or even if the battle was in full-tilt around him he seemed to have no problem in dozing off, even in the saddle. He would sleep in snatches, retiring early but being up again around midnight to begin his pacing or smoking a favorite cigar. Many were the nights the sentinel would see his tall and slender hulk pacing about his tent or poking at a campfire as he smoked.

Sherman had that natural quality possessed by all great generals and leaders of men which is the ability to inspire the complete confidence of his men in himself. From his perspective he felt it was because they knew he valued their lives as much as his own.

All in all he came to personify the man the South loved to hate, especially Georgians and Carolinians. This was not due to any defeat they suffered at his hands but for the 40 to 60 mile destructive path over 500 miles his army left behind. South Carolina especially suffered, as was intended and ruined for a quarter century after the war. His foragers called "bummers" had learned how to wreak havoc on the population in their march through Georgia and when they reached South Carolina, they applied it with full concentration.

Sherman hated to punish his men for infractions. He reasoned that fighting was the easiest part of war and that a general who continually quarrels with his men cannot be successful. You could not take the side of the citizens against

Sherman Takes Savannah

petty irregularities that happened. His response to the people was that war is war and not popularity seeking.

Sherman was totally indefatigable, always in motion and never idle. He always wanted to see first hand what was going on. This is not to say he didn't have confidence in his generals, he did. It's just that he wanted to see what they saw so he could speak knowledgably when they met. Sherman was constantly assessing the risk-reward of a situation; looking to gain grand results without paying the bloody penalty of war.

Not only was Sherman considerate of the feelings of his friends but also he would not permit ridicule of any one attached to him. This characteristic was well known to his officers. Actually, in all of his actions he was governed by a strong conscience and sense of duty that he brought to bear on things he considered. Decisions were quick whether the subject was light or important but not before he carefully weighed the arguments on both sides.

The general possessed an astounding memory. He could bring to mind prior campaigns in depth. Events, dates, names and faces remained fresh in his mind and available for immediate recall. It was said Napoleon had the same gift. Both could remember the minutest details of campaign tactics and whatever they had seen, heard or read.

The man was a social animal. When it was time to let go of the responsibilities of the hour, and he could cast them off with a great faculty, he could become one of the merriest at the party. He emanated a humorous disposition and had a cutting wit. The two combined often made him the center of attraction at any gathering. Occasionally he would get on familiar ground with others but it was rare when anyone would reciprocate in taking familiar liberties with him.

Although he conversed as freely as anyone, he was extremely reticent to discuss what was on his mind. He kept his own counsel. He was cautious but never accused of deceit or dishonesty. He displayed obvious contempt for arrogance

H. Ronald Freeman

and boasting but paid immediate tribute to merit, courage, manliness and simplicity. Once he gave his word on something it was gospel. He was a man of integrity and had an intense scorn for those who looked to profit out of the war.

Sherman was always a very approachable general with his soldiers. They affectionately called him "Uncle Billy." He was quite casual in the wearing of his uniform with his coat open at the throat and sporting a linen collar with a black cravat. He was often careless and unkempt in his dress and had a restlessness emphasized by his chain-smoking of cigars. He favored only one spur that he wore on the low cut shoes that he preferred over boots.

He rode a blaze-faced little horse named Sam. The horse possessed a very rapid walking gait much to the dismay of Sherman's staff. The general sat erect and active in the saddle. His nose twitched from long bouts of asthma and produced an effect as though he was sniffing out the trail ahead.

Whenever possible, he preferred a simple diet and was the last to complain when meals were reduced to hard tack and beef. The ordinary soldier's life in the field was preferred over the comforts of the cities. When the army was on the move he reduced his baggage to the minimum and shared with others the life of the common soldier. His staff felt few men had so harmoniously united common sense and genius as Gen. Sherman.

Sherman Takes Savannah

Atlanta to the Sea

By May of 1864, Sherman had an army approaching 100,000 troops camping around Chattanooga, Tennessee. On the other side was Gen. Joseph E. Johnston with sixty thousand rebels in his Army of the Tennessee entrenched in the hills of north Georgia. However, Union eyes were on Atlanta and Sherman cleverly slipped past the rebel army and closed in on the city. Johnston was forced to pull back toward Atlanta, giving up the high ground.

The southern troops retrenched again and again hoping the Union army would attack the high ground. Again and again they were wrong. The federals didn't take the bait and it just didn't work. Sherman continued to outflank the rebel positions and forced them to either withdraw or risk being cut off.

Southern leadership was not happy with the cat-and-mouse game being played by Johnston. Since there was no love lost between Jefferson Davis and Johnston, he was relieved

Gen. Joseph Johnston

of command and replaced by Lt. Gen. John Bell Hood, an officer known for his aggressiveness in battle. Immediately Hood went on the assault with his troops but was unable to negate the superior numbers on the Union side. The final outcome was seeing the federal troops gain a stranglehold on Atlanta in late summer of 1864. Hood was forced to abandon the city with the hope that the Union army would be foolish enough to pursue him into the mountains of north Georgia. It was not to be.

H. Ronald Freeman

In the fall of 1864 Northern morale was at an all-time low and Lincoln's defeat was a distinct possibility. Grant was at an impasse with Lee and was unable to produce any good news. So when Sherman wired to Lincoln and the world that "Atlanta is ours and fairly won," it was that victory that saved both the Republican Party and the Union war effort.

Gen. John Bell Hood

In Sherman's mind he was an angel of wrath, armed with a flaming sword, aimed at punishing people guilty of a mortal sin - that of bringing division to the Union and thus bringing war to the land. That made the war one against anarchy and he hated every act that smacked of illegality.

In early September 1864, Sherman enjoyed the adoration of the entire North. In four short months he had successfully led 120,000 soldiers across one hundred miles of hostile territory, survived numerous battles and countless skirmishes, inflicted terrible punishment on a Confederate army, and occupied the second most important city in the South - Atlanta. Any military figure would have accepted that as the pinnacle of a brilliant career, and few Americans could imagine greater success on the battlefield. But the war was not yet won, and Sherman worked relentlessly on a plan that would bring the Confederacy to its knees.

Atlanta fell in September 1864 and meanwhile Grant continued to hammer Lee in Virginia. All of this combined to signal the beginning of the end for the South. Southerners,

Sherman Takes Savannah

however, were unaware of this and continued to believe that victory was still within their grasp. That unyielding determination was now the crucial factor in the war. Northern victory required a defeat of southern will as much as a string of bloody successes in Virginia. Sherman saw his role as waging war on Confederate emotions while Grant battled the Confederate armies on the field. Together they would break the Confederacy, both militarily and psychologically; separate paths but toward the same goal.

Sherman needed to decide which direction out of Atlanta he would take. Where on the coast could supplies be most easily stockpiled for his arrival? He could head for Charleston, or Savannah, and then be in position to move north against Lee in Virginia. Or, he could march toward Albany destroying cotton as he went and also liberate the prisoners in Andersonville. This however, would hinder future movement alternatives of his army.

George Thomas

None of these options considered chasing Hood's army in order to placate Grant who wanted it destroyed before Sherman headed south on any new raid. Sherman obviously disagreed. His opinion was that chasing Hood was a waste of time. He could leave Gen. Thomas behind to deal with Hood. He believed if the war were fought in the traditional manner, it would drag on.

H. Ronald Freeman

However, if he could march his army through the heart of the South, it would be proof to the South and to the world that the North would prevail in the contest.

Sherman was convinced the move was proper and stated, "He would show the vulnerability of the South and make its inhabitants feel that war and personal ruin are synonymous." He would teach them that war would hurt each of them individually. Destruction of civilian society would convince the South to forgo anarchy for the peace, security and order of the Union.

In a telegram to Gen. Grant he said, "Until we can repopulate Georgia, it is useless to occupy it; but the utter destruction of its roads, houses, and people will cripple their military resources. I can make this march and make Georgia howl."

Sherman studied prewar census reports from each Georgia county and especially the agricultural production of each. His conclusion was if a million people find sustenance then his army wouldn't starve. He was especially keen on the types of crops and their yields in the counties between Atlanta and Savannah. He had an army to move and he needed to know the type of forage available. As a young officer, he had explored the hills, valleys and streams along his proposed route, twenty years earlier. "I knew more of Georgia than the rebs did," he said.

This was not new to him, as the same type of research had served him well between Chattanooga and Atlanta. Sherman studied the area well knowing his army would need more than his skill and energy to continue to drive to the sea.

He would be foraging through a rich agricultural area. Although cotton had been the major crop before the war, demand for food to feed the Confederate army had necessitated the increased planting of grain, corn and other vegetables. Cows, beef cattle, pigs, horses and sheep were also in abundance. Then too, he also needed to know the

Sherman Takes Savannah

potential opposition from the Southerners on his proposed march to the sea.

He was very positive in his telegram to Gen. Grant. He was training his troops in the art of living on the countryside and they were taking to it like ducks to water. "We won't starve in Georgia," said Sherman.

Gen. Grant was not totally enamored with Sherman's plan but consented if he would hold off until after the presidential election on November 8th. They were both in favor of Lincoln's re-election but wanted the issue resolved before initiating such a bold plan. It turned out to be no contest. Lincoln beat his democratic opponent, Gen. George McClellan by a substantial margin and with that news in hand, Sherman made ready to point his army toward Savannah and the sea.

On November 14, 1864. Sherman's Engineer Corps began the awaited task of destroying Atlanta. They demolished the railroad depot, roundhouse, machine shops and any other facility that might aid the Confederate war effort. During the night the heart of Atlanta became an inferno. One explosion followed another. Sparks shot skyward. The air was filled with smoke, burning cinders and buildings covering two hundred acres were in ruins or flames. Atlanta, with the exception of Richmond, had furnished more war material than any other city in the South. Now it was no longer an instrument of injury against the Union.

The army struck out for Savannah on the 15th of November to the tune of "John Brown's Body," and slowly headed southeast toward Savannah and the sea, about 250 miles away. Sherman left a day later and joined the left wing's 14th Corps.

Atlanta had been put to the torch as a final gesture before his departure. As he later recalled in his memoirs, "Behind us lay Atlanta, smoldering and in ruins, the black smoke rising high in the air and hanging like a pall over the ruined city." The army moved as four separate corps, each

H. Ronald Freeman

being made up of three divisions, with plans of living off the land and leaving smoke and devastation in their wake.

Many of his men were three-year veterans who had survived both hard fighting and disease. You could detect their confidence by their stride and appearance. They knew they would have to move rapidly and travel light. They planned to live on the country and carry only a minimum of food and nonmilitary supplies. Soldiers were to take only the bare necessities. The wounded and ill were transferred to other units and those unable to make a meaningful contribution were left behind.

They carried no unnecessary equipment to burden or slow them down. Each carried a blanket wrapped in a rubber poncho, a spare shirt and socks; canteen, haversack with coffee, sugar, salt and hard bread, cooking utensils, a tin cup hanging from the waist plus their weapon and cartridge box with 40 rounds of ammunition. The key elements were food, clothing and weapons.

He had written to Grant that Union possession of the Savannah River would be the death knell for southern independence. "If you can whip Lee and I can march to the Atlantic, I think Uncle Abe will give us 20 days leave to visit our families."

Undoubtedly there would be fighting but they expected little resistance. Primarily they intended to destroy the railroads to halt the flow of supplies to Lee's armies in Virginia. Also, they planned to strike a blow at southern morale, both army and civilian, while bleeding the rural economy.

Sherman Takes Savannah

Lieutenants and Logistics

The Union army moved very efficiently as it traversed through the state. At its head was the supreme commander, Gen. Sherman. The structure was then divided into two wings. The right comprised of the 15th and 17th Corps of the Army of the Tennessee (they had taken the names of southern states) and under the command of Maj. Gen. Oliver Otis Howard; the left consisted of the Fourteenth and Twentieth Corps of the Army of the Cumberland, renamed the Army of Georgia for the march, under the command of Maj. Gen. Henry Warner Slocum. Sherman respected both wing commanders and he held them in highest regard for their abilities as military leaders. The cavalry, under Gen. Judson Kilpatrick, also reported directly to Gen. Sherman. It contained some 244 officers and 4,672 troopers.

Within each wing, there were two corps and these in turn were subdivided into divisions and brigades. Although each wing was independent, it always marched within supporting distance of the other.

Sherman had a constant and intimate knowledge of the movement of his army that his staff thought remarkable. He obviously had a genius for strategy, but to combine this with an insight into logistical movements was rare in one man. Not many things in camp life evaded the eyes of the general. During the march he would alternate his position by riding with different corps. He was thoroughly familiar with the organization within the ranks even though it numbered over sixty thousand men. Little escaped his scrutiny, from the greatest to the tiniest detail.

Slocum on the left was an 1852 graduate of West Point and a New York native. He had resigned his active commission in 1857 and began the practice of law, but remained active in the New York militia. Initially, he saw action at the first battle of Bull Run as a colonel in the Twenty-seventh

H. Ronald Freeman

New York Militia. At that encounter he was wounded in his thigh.

In August 1861, he was promoted to brigadier general and a year later to major general. He fought again in the second battle of Bull Run and then went on to fight at Antietam. After that battle he was given command of the Twelfth Corps. Slocum was on the field at Chancellorsville, Gettysburg and Chattanooga. On the push to Atlanta from Chattanooga, he was given command of the Twentieth Corps of the Union Army.

Gen. Henry Warner Slocum

Howard on the right was an abolitionist and a deeply religious man who was tagged "Old Prayer Book" and the "Christian General" because of it. He had been an able student from Maine graduating fourth in his class of 1854 at West Point. At the outbreak of the war was serving as an instructor at West Point. As they left for Savannah Howard was 33 years old.

At the first battle of Bull Run he was a colonel of the Third Maine Volunteers. Unfortunately he suffered the fate of many federal units on that day and was driven from the field. It seemed not to matter since he was promoted to brigadier general the following September. During the battle of Seven Pines Gen. Howard was wounded in his right arm and it resulted in the amputation of that limb. Regardless, he went on to assume command of the Eleventh Corps at Antietam after his commander was wounded. He was promoted to major

Sherman Takes Savannah

general in November 1862 and fought at Fredericksburg. Afterwards he was given full command of the Eleventh Corps and saw his army routed by Stonewall Jackson at Chancellorsville in May 1863.

At Gettysburg, in the interim period between the death of Maj. Gen. John Reynolds and the arrival of Maj. Gen. W. S. Hancock, Howard was given the overall command of Union forces. In the fall of 1863, the Eleventh Corps was transferred to Chattanooga still under the command of Gen. Howard.

During the battle for Atlanta, Gen. James B. McPherson, commander of the Army of the Tennessee, was killed and Sherman assigned Howard to command that army. It was to become Sherman's

Gen. Peter Osterhaus

right wing during his march to the sea. The six commanders of his armies and corps divisions during this march only averaged 31 years of age.

The 15th Corps was under Maj. Gen. Peter Joseph (P.J.) Osterhaus. He was a veteran of the unsuccessful 1848 democratic revolution in Germany and fled to the United States to become an American citizen. He was in command of a German regiment from St. Louis and had proven himself to be a

Gen. Frank P. Blair

H. Ronald Freeman

very able leader under fire. The 15th numbered 724 officers and 14,568 men and included divisions commanded by brigadier generals Charles R. Woods, William B. Hazen, John Smith and John M. Corse.

The 17th Corps was under the command of Gen. Frank P. Blair, a three-time congressman from Missouri who was still in office. He never lost his coolness and self-assurance and it allowed him to master any situation and instill confidence in his troops. He was one of the most popular men in the army. Appearance wise he sported a red, sandy beard and mustache and he stood about an inch less than six feet. His face emanated good humor. He was an excellent horseman who always rode a superior mount. His reputation was one of a kind, discreet, generous and brave man. The 17th was the smallest corps with only 420 officers and 10,667 men. It's division generals were Joseph A. Mower, Mortimer D. Leggett and Giles A. Smith.

Maj. Gen. Alpheus S. Williams, commander of the 20th Corps, was a lawyer and had proved himself to be a competent general. He usually rode with his coat buttoned to the chin and his fat legs sticking straight out in the stirrups. His head was huge and sported a private's hat that made him look more like a country doctor battling the gout with a love of whiskey than he did a soldier.

Gen. Alpheus Williams

In the years prior to the Civil War, Williams served as a probate judge of Wayne County, president of a bank, owner of the Detroit *Advertiser*, postmaster of Detroit, and member of the Board of Education. His military activities began early in his Detroit years, when he enlisted in the local militia, the Brady Guards. "He worked

Sherman Takes Savannah

through the ranks from private in 1838 to Major General of the Michigan Militia twenty years later. Williams also served during the Mexican War.

After Gettysburg, he followed Lee's retreat into Virginia. However, in September he was ordered west to join Sherman's Army in Chattanooga following the Union disaster at Chickamauga. He fought with distinction in the Union victories at Resaca, New Hope Church, Kolb's Farm, and Peachtree Creek. At Resaca his "Red Star" division, as it was now known, fought the decisive action that lead to the Union victory. He was known as "Old Pap" because of his unusually full beard. He was beloved by his troops, highly regarded and honored by his fellow officers. The 20th Corps had 602 officers and 12,862 men with divisions headed by brigadier generals Nathaniel J. Jackson, John W. Geary and William T. Ward.

After the war Williams was appointed minister resident to El Salvador (1866-69) and then elected as a Democrat to two terms of Congress (from 1875 until his death).

Gen. Geary, commander of a division within the 20th Corps, would become the military governor of Savannah. He was tall with a full black beard and an inviting face. He was sensible and firm but with a hearty and hospitable manner.

On the left wing, the 14th Corps was under Maj. Gen. Jefferson C. Davis, not to be confused with the Confederate president. Davis' war record was admirable. He began as a 1st lieutenant at Ft. Sumter when it received the opening fire of the war. From there he was appointed a colonel of the Twenty-Second Indiana Militia and ultimately rose to brigadier general in that group by December 1861. He was said to be one of Sherman's favorites. Many felt he was too friendly with the southern ladies and he was criticized for threatening to shoot anyone caught looting during the march.

There was also the "incident." Davis had quarreled with his former commander, Maj. Gen. William "Bull" Nelson of Kentucky. The encounter took place in the lobby of the Galt

H. Ronald Freeman

House, a hotel in Louisville. Davis took issue with Nelson about a former insult and Nelson slapped his face. Davis

Typical Pontoon Bridge

responded by drawing his pistol and shooting him point blank. Nelson was killed and Davis was arrested. Fortunately for him he had close ties with Gov. Morton of Indiana and never faced charges. The matter was dropped and he was back at his command with little time lost. The 14th Corps had 556 officers and 12,397 men. Divisions were commanded by brigadier general's William P. Carlin, James D. Morgan, and Absalom Baird.

An eight-horse team drew each caisson and its accompanying gun. Rations for twenty days were carried along with two hundred rounds of ammunition per man and per major gun. Each soldier marched out with forty rounds of ammunition

Sherman Takes Savannah

and three days of rations in his pack. Marching orders changed every day with regiments rotating positions in the brigade, brigades rotating in divisions and divisions rotating within the corps.

In addition to the troops, the supply wagons numbered twenty-five hundred, each drawn by six mules, carrying a 20-day supply of hardtack, a 40-day supply of sugar, salt and coffee, and of course adequate ammunition to sustain any foreseeable firefight.

To carry the load there were 17,000 horses and mules. If the army were stretched out in a line, it would cover fifty miles and the wagons another thirty. The number of troops on the move was huge. One lady timed the passage of the army in front of her house from nine in the morning until late at night. It was a moving mass of "blue coats" marching past her home - infantry, artillery and cavalry: Infantry numbered 55,329, cavalry at 5,063 and 65 artillery guns operated by 1,812 men.

Rivers were in front of them to be forded or crossed. For that purpose, pontoons for temporary bridges had to be available. During the Union army's march there were also 1,550 men to lay pontoon bridges.

The Bummer

Each wing had 51 canvas pontoon boats that could assemble a bridge 850 ft. long. These boats plus 4,000

H. Ronald Freeman

lbs. of rope and other accoutrements for the bridges were transported in 148 wagons.

Sherman's personal staff was small, consisting of only five officers. Any important correspondence he just kept in his pockets. His saddlebags carried only the essentials; a change of underwear, cigars and of course, a flask of whiskey.

What made Sherman's western army successful while its eastern counterpart under Grant struggled in Virginia against Lee? The answer was in leadership. He made a point of weeding out the political appointees and incompetent career officers. Those left were young, talented and for the most part self taught in military matters. Many had risen from the ranks and had a special concern for the welfare of the common soldier under them.

The foreseeable as well as the unforeseeable had to be planned for. Men would get injured, wounded and sick. To address these contingencies, 300 ambulances accompanied them. Meat would be needed to feed a hungry army on the move. The general plan was to forage off the land but Sherman knew that wouldn't always be possible. To supplement the meat expected from forage, there was a herd of 3,000 cattle, following the wagons, adequate to supply an estimated forty days of beef. What forage they couldn't eat, they would destroy.

Sherman's orders to his commanders were broad. They were to sustain their armies by foraging on the land to the fullest extent possible. The standard was set of 15 miles per day to be made on the march. There was no stopping for lunch and the men ate whenever they could. The rations, although plentiful, were a reserve since the plan was for the army to live on the land.

Each brigade assigned that mission would form foraging parties. Destruction of buildings along the way would only be allowed by permission of the corps commanders. Horses, mules and wagons were to be appropriated freely. The country left behind the army was to be rendered useless by destroying

Sherman Takes Savannah

railroad tracks, mills, and factories. This meant relentless devastation was to be the norm. Each brigade appointed a foraging party of 30 to 50 men to comb the countryside under the command of an officer.

Each day before dawn they would set out several miles ahead and to the flanks and scour the plantations for livestock, corn and anything edible that could be consumed. During the day they would bring the goods back to the column in captured wagons pulled by confiscated horses. Once there the forage would be picked up by the supply wagons. These men were called "bummers" and usually rode captured horses and mules with only a rope for a rein and a piece of carpet for a saddle.

The bummers also acted as scouts in covering the front and flanks of the advancing column. It was a brilliant concept in that it protected the army from surprise and made time wasting deployments unnecessary. When they encountered rebel cavalry they drove the laden mules to the rear and immediately formed a well-concealed and extended firing line. When pressed, they made a fighting withdrawal while reinforcements rallied to their support. Many times this would give the enemy the impression they were the main line of the army.

Sherman's first problem was the weather leaving Atlanta, He had hoped to leave Atlanta after the autumn rains ended but upon leaving the city a cold drizzle began to fall. Moving the wagons, artillery and thousands of horses and mules became a severe trial. Wagons bogged down and overturned forcing men to shovel mud into the ditch and roughen the underlying roadbed with logs to provide traction when overloaded wagons became mired. When animals fell from exhaustion, they were shot and left behind leaving a clear trail of corpses. Sherman learned from the locals that this was one of the coldest Novembers in memory.

H. Ronald Freeman

Marching Through Georgia

The middle of Georgia in the fall of 1864 was viewed as a "perfect garden." Gov. Brown had urged farmers to reduce their cotton fields and plant more foodstuffs in order to supply the armies of Lee and Hood for the coming winter. Farmers obeyed and in addition their yards were filled with hogs, chickens and turkeys and the fields abounded in game. Barns were filled to capacity with shucked corn for the animals. Other grains were piled high in the lofts. Sides of meat and salted carcasses hung from the rafters while pantry shelves sagged with preserved fruits and vegetables. Sweet potatoes, always a favorite, filled the root cellars.

When foragers located a plantation they followed a pre-ordained and previously successful procedure. Quickly, they searched for rebels and if none were found, established perimeter guards for warning in case of attack. Then, they secured provisions and either found or appointed a cook to see to their needs. Lastly, they went about gathering food for their brigade. The foragers confiscated barrels of flour and cornmeal, raided the smokehouse of cured hams and bacon and gathered all the fruits and vegetables they could find.

Honey, sweet potatoes and molasses were in particular demand. Horses, mules and cattle were tied to the backs of wagons, coaches or buggies. Hogs, chickens, geese and turkeys, often caught after amusing chases, were butchered on the spot and thrown across a horse or mule. Unwanted animals were shot and left to rot on the premises.

The orders given the foragers were liberal. It was said they could gather vegetables and drive livestock to within sight of the camp. Horses and mules could be confiscated freely although there should be discrimination between the rich, who were hostile, and the poor, who were industrious, neutral and friendly. Soldiers were forbidden to enter dwellings or commit any trespass. Army corps commanders alone could authorize the only destruction permitted. Even here they had to adhere

Sherman Takes Savannah

to the general principle of refraining from destruction in areas where they were unmolested. However, the rule was if attacked or encountering bridges and roads destroyed by inhabitants, commanders were authorized to invoke a devastation of the same intensity as the hostility encountered.

A foraging party would be briefed at dawn on the route to be followed by their unit and where they would camp that evening. The party would then visit every farm within five or six miles along the path of march. It would begin by confiscating wagons and the animals to pull them. Then they would load up with feed and foodstuffs. The group would return to the army's route at some point ahead where they would deliver the day's booty to designated officers. The day's haul could be anything from ham, bacon, eggs and poultry to bags of cornmeal.

Not only foodstuffs were taken but also every imaginable thing under the sun that foolish soldiers would get in their heads to abscond with. They had pockets bulging with silver and gold coins. The men as well as the officers often wore fine jewelry along with sparkling rings.

Although Sherman acknowledged in his memoirs that the foragers committed acts of violence along with pillaging and robbery, they were incidental and not the norm. He denied any murders or rapes during the march. Although in theory he opposed plundering, it helped create the kind of terror he was attempting to instill in the population in the path of the march. The more havoc he could wreak, the less hope the civilians would have and the less trust they would place in their government and its army.

What was accomplished was the burning and destruction of hundreds of buildings along the sixty-mile wide march from Atlanta to Savannah. The cotton gins and the cotton inside were burned and the slaves encountered were freed.

H. Ronald Freeman

Making Georgia Howl

Sherman instructed his corps commanders in the art of destroying railroads in detail. "Let the destruction be so thorough that not a rail or tie can be used again." The men used tools developed by Sherman's engineer Poe. They tore up track - rails, ties and all, from the grade. The ties were stacked into waist-high piles and torched. Then the centers of the rails were placed over the fire. Once red hot, they were rendered useless by bending them around telegraph poles or trees. They became known as the legendary "Sherman's "Bowties."

His also used a grapple hook his engineers had designed, that made the rails impossible to straighten without machinery. Hundreds of miles of railroad track were wrecked and twisted in this manner.

No one in front of the army could impede them. The state was practically devoid of meaningful manpower. There were no spare troops to oppose Sherman's 15 divisions. Deciding where the army was heading was a guessing game for the few Confederate defenders. Sherman's path was

Sherman Takes Savannah

consciously set to keep the rebels guessing. His right wing under Howard, along with the cavalry, initially seemed to be heading for Macon along the Macon and Western Railroad but then actually passed north of it. His left wing under Slocum followed the Georgia Railway east toward Augusta. Sherman hoped to confuse the rebels since he was actually targeting Milledgeville, the state capital that was located between the two cities. Not being sure where the army was going made it impossible for the rebels to concentrate their defenses. Then unexpectedly to the rebels, but just as Sherman planned, both wings converged on Milledgeville.

Sherman's Bowties

Before departing to avoid the advancing army, the Georgia Legislature passed a law requiring every able-bodied citizen to rise up and defend his state. They exempted only themselves and judges from service. Then they spent three thousand dollars of the taxpayer's money to rent a train to take them away from danger. They said they were leaving for the "front" and would meet again at a time and place designated by the governor.

Gov. Brown was busy with other matters. As the troops approached Milledgeville he hurriedly went to the prison in search of recruits. Inside he assembled the 126 convicts and offered pardons to all that would join Gen. Howell Cobb's militia. Most had little to lose and accepted without hesitation. After that, Brown joined with other prominent citizens of the town in preparing for their eastward flight "to the front" by rail.

Their special train, and many wagons and buggies, was loaded with furniture, clothing, and other personal effects. Brown stripped the governor's mansion of everything except the very heavy items. Most of the furniture, bedding, curtains, carpets, a cow and the contents of his pantry, down to the last cabbage, were loaded. And at that point, the governor left town.

Arriving with the vanguard, Gen. Slocum quartered himself in the first-rate Milledgeville Hotel. Sherman, who arrived later with the 14th Corps, made himself at home in the governor's mansion. A Union soldier described it later as "the most beautifully finished-off building I ever saw." Sherman complained good-naturedly about the former occupant's lack of hospitality.

While plundering, some of the men found millions of dollars worth of unsigned Georgia Confederate currency. They used it to light their pipes and cigars. Poker games were held with million dollar stakes while some of the money was given to female factory workers, who had not been paid for months. Their windfall excited them until they realized the worthlessness of the money. Slaves fought over the bills and one was overheard to say, "Bless the Lord - we're richer than poor Massa now!"

In Milledgeville, like in Atlanta, Sherman authorized the destruction of all military material. Stores from the state magazine were dumped into the river and then the structure was blown up damaging two churches on the square in the

Sherman Takes Savannah

process. Then he torched the nearby arsenal. The state penitentiary was also burned but not by Sherman. Local residents admitted the prison fire had been set by convicts left behind by Gen. Wayne. The town meant little to Sherman. His goal was to reach the coast before his supplies ran out so after two days, he abandoned the state capital.

Gen. Beauregard, in Charleston, was under the impression that Sherman's army had gone into Tennessee pursuing Gen. Hood. It was not until the 17th of November, two days after the army departed Atlanta that he learned of the true location and direction of the march. Hood's army was 300 miles to the west and would be of little aid in opposing Sherman. However, Beauregard did send an order to Hood to dispatch a cavalry division to bolster Wheeler whose troops were already engaging Sherman's army heading out of Atlanta. Hood declined, feeling his army needed to be at full strength to oppose Union troops under Gen. George H. Thomas. That army had split off from Sherman in Atlanta.

After leaving Milledgeville Sherman swung Gen. Kilpatrick's cavalry toward Augusta to again give the impression that it was the primary target. Kilpatrick was intercepted by the Confederate cavalry under Gen. Wheeler but at the last moment was able to swerve his forces again to the southeast and elude

Braxton Bragg

H. Ronald Freeman

the rebels. This diversion by Kilpatrick gave a free passage to the federal primary columns during the second leg of their march, this time from Milledgeville to Millen.

Gen. Braxton Bragg was in command of about 10,000 Confederates at Augusta. He was convinced that attack on his city would be imminent since it was a major supplier of Confederate munitions. He was wrong. It didn't happen. Sherman never intended it to. Bragg defended his decision though, staying entrenched, idly watching, and refusing to commit his force as the Union army looted and burned and passed him on its way to the sea. Sherman had obtained a Savannah newspaper on December 2nd and he knew the rebels had scattered their forces among Macon, Augusta and Savannah.

Ironically, Bragg was one of the officers Sherman had repaid on his failed investments in San Francisco municipal bonds. On a positive note, he was also one of the ones directly responsible for Sherman's appointment as president of Louisiana State Military College. Although having different allegiances, the two men had a mutual respect for each other.

The right wing under Howard was temporarily halted at the Oconee River just outside of Milledgeville. Entrenched Rebels had dug in on the other side. When they were able to successfully cross and capture several rebel defenders, they discovered they were the convicts Gov. Brown released earlier from the state prison on the condition they fight for the Confederacy.

One person who seemed to be totally out of touch with the situation was President Jefferson Davis. He wired Beauregard that the federals may head straight for the coast, especially if they were short on supplies. He said if that was the case then Confederate forces could be focused on one object and if they were unable to defeat Sherman's army, at least they could damage it to the extent that it would be no longer an effective force.

Sherman Takes Savannah

Push to Savannah

After leaving Milledgeville, the left wing entered a new type of terrain. Rather than forests and open fields they entered woods so thick the men could scarcely move forward. The women and children in the area were pathetic and sat in front of run-down huts and had an enervated and sickly look about them. Their men had gone off to fight the war and they had been left behind. The bluecoats referred to them as "dirteaters" and they impressed the northerners as tragically backward and illiterate.

Sherman and his staff moved to join the right wing for the final push into Savannah. Many people in the state thought Sherman would fall victim to the swamps, the insects and the marshes as he neared the coastal lowlands. It was expressed that Sherman could not keep up his long line of communication and sooner or later he would have to retreat. At that time it was thought that the fate that beheld the French army retreating from Moscow would be reenacted. They even thought the Georgia militia was just waiting its chance to catch the Yankees from the rear. It was not to be, the militia was almost nonexistent. The rebel forces behind Sherman were no more menacing than those in front.

Who was left to be in front of them? Where was the opposition? The answer was in the area of need. Most of the able bodied and healthy southern men were at the front in areas where it was determined they were needed most. With Hood in Alabama and Beauregard in Charleston, the only Confederate troops left in the federals' path were a combination of boys, old men and soldiers on convalescent leave.

The militia remaining in Georgia were "cradle and grave units," men younger than sixteen and older than sixty who were exempt from the draft. There was also a hodgepodge of factory workers, city guards, and railroad patrols. All in all, they numbered about 10,000 in a ragtag army that was about as pesky to Union troops as a fly on a horse. Northern officers described the opposition they met on their march as laughable.

The only significant encounter federal troops had with rebel forces occurred at Griswoldville, about ten miles east of Macon near the Central of Georgia railway. Griswoldville was founded in 1849 by Connecticut born Samuel Griswold. The town had grown so rapidly that by 1861 it was second only to Clinton, the county seat. At the beginning of the war Griswold adapted his cotton gin to meet the needs of the Confederacy. The governor's call for military arms encouraged him to switch his production to weapons and by mid-1860 22 machines were producing a six shooter percussion cap pistol patterned on the 36 caliber Colt Navy revolver. It sold for forty dollars.

Gen. Howard put Brig. Gen. Charles C. Walcutt in command of a 1,500-man rear guard. They encountered some of Wheeler's cavalrymen, drove them off, and occupied a strong, entrenched position on a farm situated on a low hill with open fields to their front. Suddenly a force of about 1,500 Georgia militiamen charged across the open ground, supported by artillery fire. After three futile assaults they withdrew.

The federals' victory became a somber one when they inspected the dead and wounded and discovered they were only old men and boys. Estimated casualties were 62 Union soldiers and 650 Confederates. The battle was no more than carnage by a trained army over fervent but ill prepared troops. When the Union soldiers viewed the dead and wounded and saw the caliber of their opposition, many were literally sick.

Griswoldville would be one of those events that ensured a place for Sherman's name in the history books. Not much of a town survived. It was basically a factory town and those factories had turned to war production. As a result Union soldiers destroyed almost everything except Griswold's home. After Griswold died in 1867 the town all but disappeared.

Sherman Takes Savannah

The only other combat was between northern and southern cavalry. The southern mounted troops under Wheeler kept up a running battle with Kilpatrick's Yankee riders. They clashed near Waynesboro on the 27th of November and again on December 4th. Kilpatrick had been ordered by Sherman to engage the rebel cavalry at every opportunity but also to feint in his raids toward Augusta to keep the rebels guessing as to the true objective of the army.

Although he didn't show early promise as a cavalry leader, Wheeler was considered to be one of the South's finest generals in leading mounted troops. He was also one of the smallest major generals ever commissioned. He was only 5 feet 5 inches tall and weighed but 120 pounds. He was an Augusta native and graduated from West Point in 1859, just before the outbreak of the war. During his education as a cadet, some of his worst grades and experiences came from courses in cavalry tactics. Wheeler was said to be an unlikely warrior; courteous, dignified and pompous. But he was also a driving campaigner who rode farther, harder and on less food than most of his men. Early in the war he served as an artillery lieutenant. During the battle of Shiloh Wheeler lead the 19th Alabama Infantry as their colonel. Afterwards he transferred to the cavalry and rose to the rank of brigadier general. In January 1863, he was promoted to major general and given command of the Army of Mississippi.

Gen. Joseph Wheeler

H. Ronald Freeman

Wheeler was certainly no shrinking violet in combat. He was dubbed both "Fighting Joe" and the "War Child" for his daring. He was known as a serious person and his staff could not recall his ever laughing but being quite the opposite and extremely intense in all pursuits. The native Georgian was a small man who fought with reckless abandon, had a strong sense of chivalry, and when he felt an enemy had violated that code, the reaction was savage. During the battles around Atlanta, Wheeler had constantly targeted Sherman's communication and supply lines. His mounted troops were everywhere.

The diminutive warrior commanded cavalry in many major campaigns and this made him the country's acknowledged expert in covering retreats. But his most important role was in harassing the federal march to the sea, which he accomplished with such vigor that Jefferson Davis praised him for restricting Sherman's area of destruction.

The short history of the Confederacy produced many able and flamboyant cavalry leaders, and Wheeler ranks with J.E.B. Stuart, Wade Hampton and Nathan Bedford Forrest. Wheeler fought in an incredible 127 battles and skirmishes and suffered three wounds. Sixteen horses bearing him in combat were killed. The attrition rate among his staff officers was legendary with eight being killed and thirty-two wounded.

Wheeler was fully aware of Augusta's importance to the Confederate effort. Most of the south's gunpowder and weapons of every sort were manufactured there and transported directly by railroad to Lee in Virginia. Considering the loss of Atlanta's munitions producing capability, Augusta's destruction could prove fatal to the South. The Confederate cavalry chief left small contingents of cavalry under Gen. Alfred Iverson to observe Sherman's movements and took two thousand mounted riders to intercept Kilpatrick.

Each town has its legend explaining why Sherman did not destroy it but the one for Augusta is probably the best-

Sherman Takes Savannah

known. As they tell it Sherman spared the city because of his affection for Cecelia Stovall, a Georgia beauty he may have met when he was stationed in the South in the 1840s. The Stovall family lore tells that during his fight for Atlanta Sherman spared the plantation home in Cass County and sent her a note by a slave that said, "My dear madam you once said that you pitied the man who ever became my foe. My answer was that I would shield and protect you. That I have done. Forgive all else. I am but a soldier. W.T. Sherman.

What about Wheeler's Union nemesis Kilpatrick, or Little Kil as he was known to others? What was his background and ability? He was from New Jersey, born in 1836 the same as Wheeler but graduated from West Point two years later in 1861. Kilpatrick rose through the ranks to become a brigadier general in June 1863. His promotions weren't begrudged by his fellow officers and most felt he earned them.

Although capable, Little Kil had his shortcomings. He was described by Sherman as a damned fool and many knew him as a swaggering braggart and one of the army's most avid skirt-chasers. Sherman's defense of his selection of Kilpatrick was that he needed someone of that nature to command his mounted troops on their foray through Georgia. Kilpatrick's only redeeming quality was that he did not drink to excess. He was however, a very ungraceful rider and it was said he looked more like a monkey than a man on horseback.

The Confederate cavalry under Wheeler was outnumbered by its Yankee counterpart almost two to one but always gave a

Gen. Judson Kilpatrick

good account of itself. At best it fought a delaying action since it could do little to stop the federal juggernaut that was moving steadily toward the coast.

Wheeler's troops were constantly on the move and forced into foraging, much the same as their northern counterparts. This subjected them to much criticism from southern civilians and the press. Many felt they had destroyed and stolen more than the enemy and were much more ferocious. The assessment of Savannah newspapers was that they were doing little good and a great deal of harm.

Kilpatrick also experienced animosity but his emanated from within his army and especially from the infantry. Be it jealousy or just animosity, there were derisive comments about the cavalry not fighting and just being a nuisance. Kilpatrick personally was described as vain, conceited and egotistical. Add to that obnoxious, boastful, and a womanizer. All these observations were apparently well founded. Fittingly, he loved to participate in amateur theater.

KillCav was another nickname he was awarded for his impetuous attacks against Confederate forces and for long marches that fatigued his troops and their mounts. After the war, Kilpatrick was appointed U.S. Minister to Chile, where he died in 1881.

No matter how hard they tried, Union cavalry leaders simply could not match the dashing figures cut by their Confederate counterparts. Credit had to be given to Kilpatrick for trying. Kilpatrick joined the cavalry and led a famous raid on Richmond in February 1864 that failed in its objective of piercing the city's defenses to liberate Union soldiers in Libby Prison. Sent west to lead Sherman's cavalry to Atlanta, Kilpatrick was wounded in Georgia at Resaca and had returned to New York to recuperate. Upon recovery, in April 1864, he joined Sherman for the battles in Chattanooga and Atlanta. He was chosen to head the cavalry division and led Sherman's army to the coast.

Sherman Takes Savannah

Clashes between the two cavalry forces did provide most of the military action during the march to the sea. It was a slashing, vicious series of encounters, with no quarter given on either side and considerable atrocities committed by all. "There is no god in war," said a Union soldier, "It is merciless, cruel, vindictive, un-Christian, savage and relentless. It is all that devils could wish for."

The two cavalry commanders were well acquainted with each other being fellow cadets at West Point. Kilpatrick had an edge on Wheeler in academics, and the two went all-out to be ideal cadets. In 1859 Wheeler earned only six demerits; Kilpatrick had none.

Sherman's right wing also bypassed the Confederate prison at Andersonville. Gen. Hood had requested earlier that authorities remove the prisoners to the newly constructed Camp Lawton outside Millen and the notorious compound was nearly empty and therefore no longer interested Sherman. It was not in his line of March -- but Millen was. The sleepy little town of Millen lay on the railroad between Augusta and Savannah. The prison camp designed to hold 40,000 had been hastily built in September 1860 by 300 prisoners and 500 slaves. The 40 acre stockade was guarded by three forts and received its first prisoners in October. By November more than 10,000 were there in residence.

Due to the cold weather and the approach of Sherman the prisoners were ordered transferred and early in the morning of November 20th rebel guards prodded them on to open railroad flat cars. Most were headed for Savannah. Many of these prisoners would be later transferred back to Andersonville after Sherman left the state.

The conditions at Camp Lawton were horrible. When Sherman arrived there was nothing left except a sign saying, "650 buried here". This was a telling indictment of conditions in the compound used for barely a month. Every soldier who visited the stockade came away with a hardness toward the

H. Ronald Freeman

Confederacy he had never felt before. One man described it as a hideous prison pen. Even photographer George Bernard who was along on the march and had said earlier it disturbed him to see soldiers burn houses commented after he visited Camp Lawton that the punishment of civilians who supported the rebel government was justified. Angry soldiers set fire to Millen's train depot and flames spread to the town and spread to some other buildings. The two Union wings continued their advance south with Howard's right wing following the Ogeechee River and Slocum's left following the Savannah River.

Moving across Georgia's heartland, food had been plentiful with herds of cattle increasing rather than shrinking. Little hardtack had been consumed. After Millen, and on to Savannah, they entered the pine barrens. But even here, where the primary crop was normally cotton, they were saved. The fields had been converted to corn to feed the Confederate army. Now they fed the Union army instead.

As the army approached Savannah the terrain became much different. The roads ran along narrow causeways raised above the water soaked rice fields. The entire area was covered with a network of canals, dams, and flood-gates that enabled it to be flooded for growing rice but now it was used to intentionally thwart Sherman's approach.

Rice initially was a novelty to the men but it wore off quickly and they looked forward to another change. It was promised to them when they reached the coast and they looked forward to it with a new hunger. Savannah would be the Mecca for oysters; roasted, fried and stewed and they knew any battle would slow up their steady march to "Oysterland." Delays weren't acceptable.

Sherman Takes Savannah

The Southern Alamo

Savannah was braced and heavy guns were being moved into tactical positions. Wishful thinking pervaded the city. Part of that logic was that Sherman's real target was Port Royal where he would join up with naval headquarters and totally avoid a confrontation with Savannah forces.

By December 5th, no doubt was left. Union troops had taken Statesboro, about 60 miles northwest of Savannah and were closing in on the coast, coming up from the southwest. Gen. Beauregard finally admitted the worst. In his communication to Hardee he acknowledged Savannah was the obvious destination.

On December 7th, Sherman's 15th Corps crossed the Ogeechee River about 18 miles southwest of Savannah. Meanwhile the 20th Corps was moving past Springfield and Ebenezer north of the city. Soon the western part of Chatham County and parts of Bryan and Liberty counties south of the city were teeming with federal troops. They were knocking at the gate. While at Richmond Hill they captured a train carrying the president of the Central of Georgia Railroad.

Marching through middle Georgia, Sherman's army had lived on the fat of the land. Now, at Savannah's door, food was becoming a concern. It was good planning that they had driven thousands of cattle since they found the coastal area not as hospitable as the center of the state. The army had now stopped foraging and was subsisting on a cracker a day per man plus rice and beef. Grains and vegetables were hard to come by. Some of the slaves on river plantations, left behind when their owners fled, showed the troops how to construct threshing machines to husk the rice in quantity. This discovery was the salvation of the troops. They ate rice although many detested it and would not eat it again after the war.

It was critical to the march that the army be re-supplied. Ample rations were waiting offshore. The only barrier between those rations and continued sustenance by rice was the small earthen fort on the Ogeechee River below Savannah known as Ft. McAllister. The same small fort that had withstood multiple attacks by the northern ironclads.

The Ogeechee River was Sherman's only viable supply route. He had King's Ferry about 15 miles inland as a delivery point, but the river was blocked some seven miles from the Atlantic Ocean by Ft. McAllister. It had to be taken or the northern army would starve. As long as McAllister remained in Confederate possession, re-supplying would be extremely difficult if not impossible. The reduction of McAllister was an assignment that fell Sherman's right wing.

The right wing had already reached the Ogeechee. Sherman asked Gen. Howard to get a message to the Union boats blockading the coast that he was nearing Savannah and his plan was to capture that city. To make contact, a small bateau was launched at King's Ferry and began what would be a two-day trip to the sea. During that time it would have to pass under the guns of Ft. McAllister. Actually the worst part of the trip was not in evading McAllister's guns, which they were able to do at night, but sustaining a rough sea in the sound and almost capsizing before a Union boat spotted them and sent a rescue party.

The message of Sherman's arrival was relayed to Port Royal and they in turn telegraphed the news to the North. Most knew it was the beginning of the end. Sherman's army, out of communication since leaving Atlanta, had finally surfaced in good order on Savannah's doorstep. General Grant had even joked that Sherman's army is somewhat like a ground mole when he disappears under a lawn. "You can here and there trace his track but you are not quite certain where he will come out till you see his head."

In preparing for the North's arrival, the rebel army had spared nothing in strengthening McAllister against the coming Union assault. Confederate engineer, Capt. Thomas A. White, had done everything possible to reinforce the land-oriented

Sherman Takes Savannah

defenses. McAllister's original mission was to block federal ships from entering the Ogeechee River, not to repel an invasion from the land.

Since the last naval attack in 1863, Major Anderson and the troops had worked diligently at improving Ft. McAllister's defenses. The area facing the rear had been enclosed with a high earthen wall. A deep ditch was also dug outside the fort along with a series of abitis and even a palisade of sharp stakes. The trench was fifteen-feet-deep and seven-feet-wide and its sides were almost vertical. In the center of the ditch was a thick line of sharply pointed logs, six feet high and projecting outward.

Marshes and streams protected the fort's flanks and, unknown to federal forces, Anderson had land mines thickly sown on the outer area of the fort some three feet apart and buried just beneath the surface.

The defenders, with the felling many trees and clearing the brush, had opened a field of fire against oncoming attackers. However, rather than removing the felled trees, they left them where they lay, possibly as an obstruction. What they didn't count on was that the Union troops would use them as cover as they assaulted the fort.

McAllister's obstacles were formidable indeed for the infantry to overcome, but if they were able to gain the fort, it was small and defended by only a skeleton force. On a positive note for Sherman, the largest guns faced the river and were useless against an attacking land force. The rear guns were unprotected by earthworks.

Sherman was impatient to take McAllister. It was now isolated from its Confederate pulse and surrounded by the Union army. It was on its own. What Sherman didn't know was the position the fort's commander would take regarding surrender.

From Anderson's standpoint he knew he might be in for a protracted siege. Neither reinforcements nor supplies would

H. Ronald Freeman

be forthcoming. Knowing this, the garrison had brought in provisions to support it for about 45 days. By his estimate he held over two thousand pounds of bread, forty gallons of molasses, a thousand pounds of bacon and an ample supply of salt.

As commander, Anderson had cast his lot. He and his men would defend the fort to the ultimate. From this decision there remained only two options: death or capture. He knew he couldn't expect reinforcements from any quarter and knew the odds against him were overwhelming. It was just a question of time. He only had about 150 men able to defend. The choices were simple; defend and face death, or surrender and face captivity. Unlike Ft. Pulaski earlier in the war, they would defend.

McAllister's men were tired. For days they had toiled at readying their defenses. The fort was not designed to resist a land attack from the west. It was a river battery and had proven its mettle on that field by withstanding repeated attacks of ironclads as well as gunboats. Much though had been accomplished in a short period. Guns had been relocated, abitis built and much of the open field had been mined.

To test the strength of the fort, Sherman asked Kilpatrick to go forward and see if he could open a communication with the federal fleet offshore. Kilpatrick's mounted

Gen. William Hazen

Sherman Takes Savannah

troops engaged in a few skirmishes but succeeded in driving the rebel pickets back into the fort after a few encounters. He thought, and suggested to Sherman, that he should allow him to use his cavalry and their Spencer rifles to rush the fort. Sherman declined. He had another idea on how he wanted to proceed.

He knew the weakness of the fort lay in it's exposed rear. He selected Gen. William B. Hazen's division to make the assault on the fort.

Hazen was 34 years old and a Vermont native having graduated from West Point in 1855 and had served in the northwest and in Texas. During the war had seen action at Chickamauga, Knoxville, Chattanooga and Atlanta. He had been commanding the 2nd Division of the 15th Corps of the Army of the Tennessee since August 1864. Hazen was squarely built, a little above medium height with a rugged face. He was a confident, accomplished and refined gentleman. On the field of battle he was self-assured, concentrated, brave and capable.

Hazen's division was made up of the troops Sherman commanded at Shiloh and Vicksburg. Its makeup was three brigades comprising about 4,300 men. Sherman knew what they could do and had full confidence in their ability to do it.

Hazen's men were currently on the north side of the Ogeechee River at King's Ferry and bridge. The rebel army had burned the bridge there but federal engineers had rebuilt it in three days. One day after completion, December 13th, Hazen and his men crossed. Sherman gave him the orders personally; attack McAllister with no delay.

Hazen's troops looped around and approached McAllister from the south. This enabled them to avoid the fort's guns. By 8 a.m. he was close enough to begin deploying his men. Meanwhile Sherman and Gen. Howard and staff officers went to a two-story rice mill on the north side of the river and about two miles east of McAllister to observe the action. He

H. Ronald Freeman

also planned to use the location for signaling the Union fleet offshore which he did soon after they ascended to the roof.

Sherman gave the signal to Hazen to take the fort before nightfall. He knew the odds were on his side and didn't see any problem with overrunning the stronghold. There was no reason to wait. He then received a signal from a Union vessel offshore in response to their earlier signal and asking who they were. "Gen. Sherman," was the answer. The ship then asked if McAllister had been taken. Laconically, Sherman replied, "Not yet, but it will be in a minute."

As an incentive to take the fort before dark the men were told that upon its capture they would get something worthy to eat. These were troops that had been on a sustenance diet of rice, rice, and more rice - morning, noon and night since they arrived in the coastal area.

The situation was a scene reminiscent of the Alamo in San Antonio during the Mexican War. McAllister's garrison was 150 men opposing an attacking force of 4,300 under Gen. Hazen. And of course behind this body was the northern army approaching 60,000.

As Hazen's men neared to within several hundred yards of the fort they began deploying throughout the difficult terrain. Hazen decided against demanding a formal surrender of the fort from Maj. Anderson. He felt it would only reveal his tactics and allow Anderson to give a reply filled with bravado. Meanwhile his snipers advanced and began their deadly work of picking off the men from the fort's gun crews.

Within the fort, Maj. Anderson was on his own. Gen. Hardee had not responded with any direct orders as to what should be done in face of the threat. Hazen had not sent a surrender demand and Anderson had already decided he would not surrender. He knew he was facing overwhelmingly odds but the fort would have to be taken. They would not lie down and let them have it.

He also knew there was no chance of prevailing and the fighting would become desperate. He told the assembled

Sherman Takes Savannah

garrison that the married men and older soldiers should step aside and let the younger single men handle the fighting. Everyone in the fort knew the odds. One hundred and fifty facing over four thousand.

The afternoon was growing late and shadows were starting to lengthen. The December chill was pervading the air. Sherman was determined for the assault to be made that day. The bugles sounded for assembly and it was only a short time later that Hazen shouted, "Sound the Forward!" It was four o'clock. The Union line sprang forward like a wave rolling to the shore. Immediately, there was a furious burst of fire from within the fort.

H. Ronald Freeman

Ft. McAllister Under Attack

    Felled trees left by the rebels clearing the land, provided valuable cover for the Yanks and their snipers targeting the rebel guns. Many of the big guns had been silenced but those still operating were firing furiously while streams of lead poured from the smaller guns. The worst part of it for the advancing federal troops was the series of land mines that had been planted on the landward approach to the fort. These were primitive but detonated by the weight of the men as they advanced. The result was predictable and grisly. The unfortunates were virtually blown apart. The hidden land mines exploded without warning and hurled mangled bodies into the air.
    Confederate defenders returned fire as actively as they could but the federal firepower was overwhelming and just too much for them. Federal troops moved in a slow organized and

Sherman Takes Savannah

steady line toward the fort. Hazen's men scrambled through the abatis and approached the ditch with a steady and measured step. Smoke from the cannon was everywhere but still the line moved steadily forward. Paths were made through the abitis and bridges were hastily constructed over the ditch. Since the tide was out they were even able to skirt around the defenses to the river and by doing so evade some of the firing from the palisade. In other areas they halted momentarily to yank out enough stakes to make a wide gap, through which the remainder swarmed.

Rebel guns fired crashing salvos that tore gaps in the Union line, and smoke hid the advancing soldiers from view. Sherman turned away from the scene as if unable to bear the suspense, and his officers impulsively clutched one another's arms while they peered intently at the distant, darkening battlefield. "They have been repulsed," cried one officer. But no, without faltering or fluttering, the wave rolled inward over the abitis and ditches until it finally broke on the fort itself.

In a short time, the Yankees reached the walls and were engaging in hand-to-hand combat with the determined defenders. Then it was on to the parapets. It was a face-off between determination and overwhelming odds and both sides knew the outcome was a fait accompli from the beginning. The fighting was more than fierce. It was an indescribably desperate brawl involving bayonets, rifle butts, and fists and choking. Each man had to be overcome on an individual basis.

Hundreds of soldiers tumbled into the ditch and tore paths through the palisade, braving a galling fire from rebels on the parapet above. Federals streamed through the gaps and clawed up the opposite slope, rifles in hand. Soldiers screamed as they stepped on torpedoes and were flung high into the air by the terrible explosions, but their comrades reached the top and fell on the enemy. Rebels fired their cannon until the Yankees were among them, then swung cannon ramrods until they were shot, bayoneted, or clubbed to the ground.

H. Ronald Freeman

After yielding the walls to the Yankees, the rebel defenders retreated further into the fort, still unwilling to surrender, and the melee continued. It was desperate and heroic and fought mostly with bayonets. A sea of blue uniforms clashed with a wall of gray. On the parapets severe hand-to-hand fighting was taking place. Federal flags appeared but disappeared just as rapidly. The southern defenders were fighting like rabid dogs in defense of an impossible cause.

Grudgingly the Confederates fell back into the fort's interior and fought with rifles and pistols. The men were finally forced into the bomb proofs, where they were rooted out one by one. The "fort was never surrendered," Anderson proudly declared. "It was only captured by overwhelming numbers." The assault lasted only fifteen minutes. As battles went, the assault of Fort McAllister was hardly a blur, but rarely was the gallantry of soldiers, blue or gray, more apparent.

Probably the epitome of the struggle was characterized by the brawl of the two captains, one north and the other south. The combatants were Captain Nicholas B. Clinch, McAllister's artillery commander and Captain Stephen Grimes of the 48th Illinois. The firing had ceased and the battle was over and decided but not with them. It was actually a sword-fight and both were very proficient in the art. Soldiers from both sides gathered around to watch and let them fight it out.

Clinch, when summoned to surrender by the federal captain, responded by dealing him a severe blow on the head with his saber. Captain Clinch had previously received two gun shot wounds in the arm. Even with his wounds, immediately hand-to-hand fighting ensued. Grimes was getting the worst of it and had sustained several serious wounds about his head and shoulders when fellow yanks intervened and subdued Clinch.

Federal privates came to the assistance of their officer, but the fearless Clinch was willing to continue although he was bleeding from eleven wounds (three saber wounds, six bayonet wounds, and two gun shot wounds), from which, after severe

Sherman Takes Savannah

and protracted suffering, he barely recovered. His conduct was so exemplary, and his cool bravery so much admired, as to elicit the praise of the enemy and even of Gen. Sherman himself.

Like the Alamo in Texas, the battle lasted only a few minutes. Soon after the bugle sounded the call to charge, it was over. The Alamo had been taken in 20 minutes with 189 against Santa Anna's four thousand. McAllister fell in 15, with 150 against four thousand. In each case, the courage of the defenders was outstanding.

But, the toll was bloody. Most of the Union casualties were the result of the explosions from mines buried around the fort. Union casualties were 24 killed and 110 wounded; the Confederates 17 killed and 31 wounded, or one-fifth of the garrison. Federals captured twenty-four guns and one mortar, sixty tons of ammunition, a large amount of food, and assorted arms and supplies. The victors were particularly joyous over a cache of wine they considered priceless regardless of the value,

To make it official the Confederate flag was lowered and the Stars and Stripes hoisted in its place. The interior of the fort was strewn with the bodies of dead Confederates who scorned surrender. They lay alongside their Yankee counterparts.

Sherman couldn't contain his exuberance. His message to Gen. Slocum was ecstatic. "Take a big drink, a long breath and then yell like the devil." Sherman said "It was the handsomest thing I have seen in this war". His officers said they had never seen the general in such a good mood. As he shared a boat with others on the way to McAllister, he even joined in many of the songs being sung by the troops. He joined Gen. Hazen with fellow officers and his prisoner Maj. Anderson for dinner in a house near the fort, formally occupied by the overseer of McAllister plantation.

H. Ronald Freeman

Anderson knew Sherman and his staff were fond of good cigars and offered them Cuban Havana's from his personal stock. Sherman, relishing in the moment replied, "Thank you major but I have some very good ones of my own." With that he offered Anderson one of Anderson's own captured cheroots.

Sherman Takes Savannah

Sherman was amused when the black waiter turned out to be a former slave owned by Maj. Anderson's family. Anderson was visibly surprised and asked, "What are you doing here Jim?" The waiter replied, "I'm working for Gen. Hazen now." Sherman more than appreciated Anderson's incredulity. Sherman let Anderson know his feeling about

Clearing Ft. McAllister of Mines

using the land mines against his men. "Men who set the mines are always elsewhere at detonation and the use of this weapon was cowardly, barbarous and inhumane." He told Anderson he was considering taking a body of southerners, including Anderson, equal in number to the men he lost to their mines, locking them up and blowing them up with gunpowder. Although he didn't carry out his threat, he used southern prisoners to clear the area of mines.

H. Ronald Freeman

To his mind, it was equitable. The land mines needed clearing and Sherman felt he knew the ones who should be responsible for the duty. He called for work details of southern captives to clear the remainder of the mines surrounding the fort. To this Maj. Anderson objected vociferously, saying this treatment of his men was unwarranted. Sherman wasn't moved and continued to let the southern prisoners search for the mines. Over the next few days, work parties of Confederate prisoners explored any disturbed patch of ground for torpedoes, which were carefully removed. Fortunately, no one was injured.

Sherman sent messages to Washington including one to Secretary of War Stanton saying that all the southern threats to head off and starve his army were just that – threats, and empty ones at that. His army was in good condition and ready and he felt Savannah was as good as taken.

With the Ogeechee River now open provisions began to flow. Sherman set large details to work building a wharf, warehouse and depot at King's Ferry to receive the guns, equipment and supplies from Port Royal. The Union army now had an open line to the sea for provisions and its base of operations near the city.

Sherman garrisoned the fort with three hundred men and made ready for when he would eventually turn north and invade the Carolinas. Ft. McAllister's guns were dismantled to be carried north as trophies of war.

A plan was worked out with the Union blockade offshore to supply the army and the obstructions in the Ogeechee River were cleared so the Union transports could begin supplying food, clothing and even mail upriver to the troops. Overrunning the fort meant what was good for the goose was bad for the gander. The fall of McAllister meant that the back door to Savannah was open and the Yankees were using it to bring in the heavy artillery for use in the reduction of the town. Gen. Hardee wired President Davis on the 15th of December

Sherman Takes Savannah

that unless reinforcements were forthcoming he would have no choice but to evacuate the city.

H. Ronald Freeman

The Noose Tightens

To seize Savannah without an assault required Sherman to accomplish two things. The first was to establish communications with the Union blockading fleet and open a supply base. A stationary army in a siege situation quickly runs out of supplies and consumes all the food available locally. The first of those things was accomplished with the fall of McAllister.

The second goal was to completely surround the city. The offshore blockade had effectively isolated Savannah from the east three years earlier, and Sherman's forces sealed the city from the south and west.

Hardee would have abandoned the city before Sherman's arrival if it had not been for a road called the Union Way. That road lay on the Carolina side of the Savannah River, opposite Sherman's army and the city. If Hardee could transport his forces across the river, he could march to Hardeeville and from there board trains for Charleston.

The southern army knew Sherman was coming but did not know his total strength or his plan of assault. Hardee's small force still crouched behind Savannah's entrenchments, but now Sherman had a secure supply line and could take his time in squeezing the rebels out. However, he was shaken from his happy complacency by a letter from Gen. Grant saying, "Forget about Savannah. Make a secure base on the ocean and leave a strong enough garrison to support it and bring the rest of your command here by water with all dispatch. I have concluded the most important operation toward closing the rebellion will be to close out Lee and his army."

Sherman was disappointed. He had his heart set on the capture of Savannah. He knew it was practical and so near at hand.

Sherman didn't want to go and again resume a part in the conventional war but an order was an order and he was a soldier and he was required to obey. He began preparing McAllister as the base that Grant envisioned. Since he

Sherman Takes Savannah

expected a fleet of a hundred ships to eventually arrive and transport his force north, he prepared Ft. McAllister as a staging area. He also knew it would take some time to assemble the necessary ships to transport his army so he felt he still had time to capture Savannah before they arrived. Sherman estimated he could reach Grant in six weeks.

He told his generals, "If Gen. Hardee is alarmed, or fears starvation, he may surrender; otherwise I will bombard the city. I will not risk the lives of our men by assaulting across the narrow causeways. If I had time, Savannah -- would surely fall into our possession."

Sherman believed Hardee could not feed the garrison and citizens for longer than a few days. "The only passage from the city available to Hardee," Sherman declared, is a disused wagon road. I could easily get possession of this." He felt however, it was not worth isolating a force across the Savannah River.

.Although he was a soldier, Sherman had objections, strong objections, to Grant's plan. He was on the doorstep of Savannah and had fixed his eye on its capture since leaving Atlanta. He was not about to pull out without an argument and leave the climax of his march to the sea to someone else. He was also convinced that his mission was among the civilian population rather than joining Grant in Virginia against Lee. He thought the destruction of railroads and depriving the Confederate army of food and supplies while striking fear into the heart of the people would prove far more effective in destroying morale, and therefore the South.

His plan was to continue to thrust the Union army sword of destruction into the Carolinas but even more so than he had in Georgia. He knew he needed to respond to Grant with an argument that would allow him to continue on his original fiery path.

While continuing preparations for a sea journey to Virginia as ordered, Sherman hoped for time to subdue Savannah. "With Savannah in our possession, at some future time if not now, we can punish South Carolina as she deserves," Sherman wrote to Grant, "and as thousands of the people in Georgia hoped we would do. I sincerely believe that the entire country, North and South, would rejoice to have this army turned loose on South Carolina, to devastate that state in the manner we have done in Georgia, and it would have a direct and immediate bearing on your campaign in Virginia."

Sherman received the news of Confederate Gen. Hood's defeats in Franklin and Nashville and knew the southern cause in the western theater was doomed. Meanwhile Sherman convinced Grant to let him march his army overland to Virginia rather than be transported in ships. He argued it would be quicker and his men would be in better condition because of it rather than being cooped up in cramped quarters.

If Union forces occupied the Union Way or the railroad across the river, Hardee would be trapped, and Sherman's future course through the Carolinas would be virtually unopposed. Preventing Hardee's escape would be the job of Gen. Slocum's left wing assisted by Gen. Foster's force at Hilton Head that later proved to be ineffectual.

* * * * * * * * * * *

In Savannah, after the offshore blockade was in place and Pulaski fell, there had been the constant fear of attack and occupation from the sea. The city had been braced for that invasion. Finally, it was coming but from a totally different direction. Eyes had turned from east to west. If they could have seen into a distance they would have witnessed the billowing clouds of black smoke from destroyed farmhouses as the Union army lumbered forward. The word was out. Sherman was coming.

Through word of mouth, the people had known what was approaching. The slaves had become fractious and worked as little as possible. All of their talk was centered on

Sherman Takes Savannah

liberation. Ads had appeared in the newspapers offering to sell large quantities of slaves at bargain prices. Outgoing trains, away from the invasion, were loaded with families, property and other valuables while inbound trains carried mostly northern prisoners being transferred in from other points.

Like most of Georgia, Savannah had been stripped of able-bodied men. Gen. Lafayette McLaws, now in command of one of the town's divisions, only fielded 1,800 troops. Every man, who could, was serving at the front. Gen. Lee said from Virginia that every available man in the South who could be, should be sent to Savannah. Let no man refuse. Even those who had been confined to barracks for disciplinary reasons were released and ordered to rejoin their units. In spite of all these efforts the total force mustered at Savannah was less than 10,000 men.

Confederate Gen. William Hardee waited. Savannah lay only a dozen miles ahead of the Union army. Marshes, rice fields and canals guarded its approaches. Sherman was confined to five narrow causeways that led through this watery wilderness like spokes leading to a hub. These spokes consisted of three roads and two rail lines, all of which could easily be defended by being swept with artillery from Confederate guns.

Sherman pushed his troops closer and closer in a slow and deliberate pincer movement forming a siege line across those spokes that was shaped like an irregular crescent. Sherman's new position was only four miles from the heart of the city and was established with no resistance from the defenders. They only watched. From their concealed positions they defended a system of earthen forts and rifle pits behind rows of pointed logs and flooded lowlands. Most of these areas could be flooded or drained at will by lowering or raising the floodgates. The Confederates knew a frontal assault along this line against them was all but impossible. Sherman's left was planted three miles above the city on the Savannah River

H. Ronald Freeman

and his right at King's Ferry on the Ogeechee River. On December the 10th one of Sherman's officers complained, "How long will it take us to get over the last five of our 300 mile march."

With the capture of Savannah, the march through Georgia would be complete. The state had been ransacked. The Confederacy had been deprived of its natural resources, not only its crops, but its cattle, horses and mules along with 265 miles of railroad being destroyed and twisted useless. In addition, the moral damage was incalculable. Sherman had pierced the heart of the South and demonstrated to all that the Confederate army was in no position to prevent it.

No longer would southerners lend credence to the confident assurances of their leaders and newspapers. Theirs had been a loss of faith that leads to a loss of hope and ends in the lack of the will to fight. Sherman had learned in his West Point ethics class that war was fought between people, not armies. During his numerous assignments and travels throughout the South, he had come to like the people and recognize their prideful stubbornness. He knew it would require enormous bloodshed and total victory to force them to give up their war effort.

Based on the early years of the war, these lessons were corroborated. Sherman believed the South would fight to the bitter end by any means available. He believed the war effort had to be total in order to convince the South to quit. More slaughter on the battlefields was not the answer. Rather, destruction of Southern land and property to break their will made much more sense.

Sherman's march to the sea was one of the major events of the Civil War. The Confederacy could not prevent the Union army from moving unimpeded through its heartland, destroying everything in its path, taking its food and personal goods, freeing its slaves, terrorizing its people and shaming its military in the field. Its days were numbered. Sherman arrived

Sherman Takes Savannah

on the outskirts of Savannah with his army in better shape than when it left Atlanta.

H. Ronald Freeman

Yankees at the Gate

Savannah could feel the hot breath of Sherman's army approaching. The town was nervous and panic was setting in. Caissons of artillery were rolling throughout the town into pre-ordained positions and there was yelling, profanity and screaming everywhere. Cotton, destined for English mills, was rotting on the docks, unable to evade the blockade and therefore worthless to the owners.

There were multiple canals that were used to flood the pervading rice fields. These, once flooded gave two to four feet of water in much of the approach to the city. Breastworks mounted with batteries defended the major highways and railroads. The perimeter battle line of the city was guarded by 54 heavy guns and these were supplemented by 11 field batteries consisting of 48 guns.

Gen. William Hardee

Mayor Richard Arnold called for all able-bodied men to take up arms and defend their town. He felt the city was well fortified and those positioned behind substantial entrenchments could repel a force greatly outnumbering their own. His was a call in vain. Savannah's able-bodied men were already in service with Lee in Virginia or some other active front.

Commodore Tattnall, now back on duty in Savannah, saw the need to destroy shipyards and where necessary the vessels under construction so as not to fall into enemy hands. Sailors on board active vessels would be redeployed in the trenches if necessary.

Sherman Takes Savannah

The clarion call had gone out in the Confederacy - Defend Savannah. Bragg, knowing that Sherman no longer was threatening Augusta, sent three thousand troops by rail to reinforce Savannah.

The enemy was getting into the act as well. Union Gen. John Foster had been trying to sever a vital rail line that linked Savannah and Charleston about 30 miles north of Savannah. His troops were a combined Union force numbering about 5,000 and made up of soldiers, sailors and marines based at Port Royal. They knew if they could sever the rail line between Charleston and Savannah it would cut the supply line and communications between the two coastal cities and perhaps force Hardee to retreat immediately from Savannah.

Foster's pathetic attempts so far had federal and Confederate officers alike ridiculing his military abilities; In spite of the criticism and because Sherman's advance had inspired him, he marched a division from Hilton Head to break the railroad. If his effort was successful, the Confederates would be penned up in Savannah.

Fortune smiled on Hardee in the guise of Maj. Gen. Gustavus W. Smith commanding 1,000 troops of the Georgia militia. While Sherman marched closer, the Georgia militia took a circuitous journey. After the massacre at Griswoldville, Smith's men were dispatched to Savannah in a roundabout manner. They left Macon on the morning of November 25th for a 100-mile ride to Albany, where the rails terminated on the Southwestern line. From there the men marched to Thomasville, covering the 60 miles in 54 hours, and arrived at noon on November 28th.

At Thomasville, Smith was angered to find only two of the five trains he requested. Because of the condition of Georgia's rolling stock, those two trains could carry only one brigade and did not arrive at the outskirts of Savannah until 2:00 a. m. on November 30th. The officers and men were "broken down by fatigue and want of rest," Smith wrote.

H. Ronald Freeman

Smith left his men on the train and rode into Savannah to report his presence to Gen. Hardee. At that hour of the night Smith found Hardee in bed. Smith was met by what he considered to be an outrageous request. Hardee ordered Smith to immediately proceed into Carolina to intercept the Union forces planning to attack the rail line. Smith balked. He couldn't believe he was being asked to take Georgia troops away from the state.

He reminded Hardee of the old decree from Gov. Brown prohibiting troops from leaving the state without an act of the legislature. Smith declared: "You know the militia of this state cannot be legally ordered beyond its borders without a special act the legislature. But if you can satisfy me that it is absolutely necessary that my command go into South Carolina, I will make every effort to carry out your orders. If you do not satisfy me, and persist in your orders, I will be under the disagreeable necessity of withdrawing the state forces from your control."

Fortunately, Gen. Hardee, Gen. Richard Taylor, and Robert Toombs together were able to convince Smith that the situation was dire indeed and it was imperative that he and his troops leave Georgia and oppose the federals in South Carolina. With that, the Georgia militia aboard the trains headed for the river.

Although a number of Smith's enlisted men complained of the mission, his officers were supportive. So before the trains actually reached Savannah, they were switched onto the Charleston line, and Smith's exhausted men awoke in South Carolina. Gen. Taylor quipped that they were "unconscious patriots." It has been suggested by many historians that the Confederacy died because of states' rights, and this incident is a classic example of state interest versus the Confederate cause.

The federal division, led by Gen. John R. Hatch, failed to reach the railroad on November 29th. He blamed inaccurate maps and worthless guides, but his own

Sherman Takes Savannah

competence seemed to be in question as well. Smith's militia arrived in time to join other outnumbered Confederate troops and defend the rail line in what became known as "The Battle of Honey Hill." Few had any sleep after a lurching train ride through the night.

Early on the morning of November 30th the Georgia militia deployed east of the railroad near Honey Hill, South Carolina. They received excellent supporting fire from a battery of South Carolina artillery, which was able to sweep a narrow causeway over which the federals had to advance. When Hatch attempted a flanking maneuver, the Georgians set fire to a dry field of broom sedge. According to federal Gen. Jacob Cox, "this prairie fire sweeping down before the wind upon our troops forced them to seek cover in a ravine."

The federals regrouped and forced the Confederates back to a ridge where a fort with seven mounted cannon guarded all approaches. The Yankees charged this position repeatedly throughout the afternoon, but Smith's men, firing rapidly from their rifle pits, and the Confederate artillery soundly repulsed every attack.

Some of the militia boys were so young they couldn't see over the fortification parapets in order to fire their weapons. They resolved this by taking turns squatting on their hands and knees and allowing their fellow troops to use their backs and shoulders as firing platforms. They acquitted themselves well.

Hatch disengaged at dark and retreated, leaving the railroad firmly in Confederate hands. Smith had lost only eight men with 42 wounded, while Union casualties were staggering.

For a small battle, there was immense slaughter. This time around it was the Yankees whose bodies covered the ground after several futile assaults through a swampy expanse covered with trees and brush. A Union soldier was quoted as saying "we fought in dense woods and marsh and it was almost impossible to maneuver more than half our troops." After the

H. Ronald Freeman

fighting ended a southerner claimed that outside the rebel earthworks he saw some 60 or 70 bodies in a space of about an acre. Many horribly mutilated by the shells. For the Union it was Griswoldville in reverse. 750 soldiers were dead or wounded. Most of the casualties were from the Union black units in the battle.

After repulsing the Union attack the men returned to Savannah to join Hardee's other forces defending the city. Gen. Smith was able to return secure in the knowledge that his men had redeemed themselves for the slaughter suffered at Griswoldville.

In spite of Honey Hill, from the Union side everything was fine. Weather was good, roads were passable and all things seemed to resolve in their favor. Sherman was in high spirits. The only thing he found not to his liking was the abundance of buried torpedoes that he considered one of the most cowardly weapons devised on either side. It was actually a buried artillery shell with a makeshift detonator that exploded when stepped upon. It was a primitive early version of a land mine. He was of the opinion that their use was more in line with murder than war.

Richard Taylor

Like a giant anaconda, Sherman's troops were closing in to encircle the city. Lt. Gen. Richard Taylor, son of Zachary Taylor, had come to Savannah from Macon to inspect the defenses. After doing so he telegraphed Gen. Lee

Sherman Takes Savannah

that the city could not be defended with Hardee's small force. He recommended that the Confederates evacuate and march northward to join other troops in the Carolinas in opposition to Sherman should he turn in that direction.

Hardee's obvious problem was one of manpower, or the lack of it. A system of trenches had been devised and dug around the city but there were two problems with this. The first was that he didn't know from which direction the attack would come, since they were surrounded on three sides. Secondly, he only could muster about 10,000 men for defense including available militia units. If Sherman elected to put the city under siege, a third problem could arise and that was that he only had provisions for about a month.

All the while Sherman continued to tighten the coils around the city. Hardee was on the horns of a dilemma; deploy the troops and try to save the town knowing reinforcements would not be forthcoming or, save the troops to fight again and forfeit the town to the federals. He wired Beauregard for his input. The order came down that if a choice had to be made between the troops and the town, then sacrifice the town. The soldiers were more important to the war effort than the citizens. The Confederate government also supported Beauregard's decision. They expressed hope that

Gen. Lafayette McLaws

H. Ronald Freeman

the town could be defended but not at the expense of the garrison. The same logic would apply to Charleston if the time came and the same situation arose.

Still, Beauregard knew if he planned to hold Savannah the rail line to Charleston would have to be kept open. The problem was that the trestle crossing of the Savannah River was too far up river to be defended. Hardee decided to pull back his guard and destroy the bridge. He dispatched his gunboats upriver to complete the job.

Actually Sherman beat him to it and was able to torch the bridge with little resistance from southern troops. Hardee still had his trump card to play. There was a plank road on the Carolina side, known as the Union Causeway, running northward to intersect the rail line. He planned for this road to be his ultimate escape hatch and godsend.

His greatest fear was that Sherman would counter his move and position federal troops on the Carolina side of the river to sever the plank road. In anticipation of this he ordered part of Wheeler's cavalry, accompanied by light artillery, to defend the road against possible threat. If the road was cut his back-door escape route was shut. Sherman countered his move by positioning a regiment of northern troops on Argyle Island in the middle of the river. This would be used as his staging area and as a quick retaliation if Hardee tried to escape.

Confederate gunboats were of no consequence in slowing Sherman. Other than the *Isondiga*, the others carried too deep a draft to allow them to steam upriver. The *Isondiga* could and although it was ineffectual, the threat of it convinced Sherman not to send troops to the Carolina side where they ran the risk of being cut off.

Sherman's attack force was positioned primarily on the west side of the city stretching from the Savannah River to the Ogeechee Canal. The left wing was still on the left near the river and the right wing being positioned near the canal. The 14th Corps was commanded by Maj. Gen. Jefferson C. Davis

Sherman Takes Savannah

and the 20th by Brig. Gen. Alpheus S. Williams. The 17th Corps was commanded by Maj. Gen. Francis P. Blair and Maj. Gen. Peter J. Osterhaus commanded the 15th.

On the Confederate side the army was organized into three divisions under Gen. Hardee. All were commanded by major generals and by name they were Gustavus W. Smith, Lafayette McLaws and Ambrose R. Wright. Former Savannah mayor, Charles C. Jones, now a colonel, commanded the artillery.

Smith and the Georgia Militia numbering two thousand men armed with twenty cannon held a position covering a two and one-half mile front from the Savannah River inward. Smith was 43 years old and a native of Kentucky. He was an 1842 graduate of West Point graduating eighth in his class of 56 and had served with distinction in the Mexican War. He taught for a short period at West Point but resigned in 1854 and worked as a civil engineer. When war erupted he was the street commissioner of New York City. He received a commission as major general in the Confederate army. His most memorable hour came in 1862 when Gen. Joseph Johnston was wounded at the battle of Seven Pines during the Peninsula campaign. At that time he briefly assumed command of the Confederate Army but an attack of paralysis, a mysterious recurring malady that occasionally rendered him unfit for duty, forced him to pass the army to Robert E. Lee. Some said that this undiagnosed disorder was brought home by knowing he could never live up to his own grandiose boasts. He was described as tall, burly and unashamedly smug. He was convinced that the Confederacy did not appreciate his abilities. Upon recovery, he served briefly as Secretary of War but did not get along with President Davis and was thrown into the Beauregard camp where he was a volunteer aide-de-camp before becoming a major general of the Georgia Militia in 1864. His actions during the Atlanta campaign brought neither recognition nor censure but he seemed to function well enough when he was not the lead commander. He had handled himself well in the recent battle at Honey Hill in Carolina.

McLaws anchored the center of the line with Wright to his left and Smith to his right along the River. McLaws commanded the next three and three-quarter miles, holding the vital center with Hardee's four thousand most experienced soldiers and twenty-nine pieces of artillery. McLaws was Hardee's most seasoned commander with experience at Gettysburg and many other battles with the Army of Northern Virginia.

He attended the University of Virginia before graduating from West Point in 1842. He was a career army officer but resigned to join the Confederate Army when the war broke out. He began his Confederate service as a colonel in the 10th Georgia Infantry. Based on his performance in the Peninsula campaign he was promoted to major general in May 1862. He fought successfully at Antietam, Fredericksburg, Chancellorsville, and Gettysburg. At Gettysburg he had a quarrel with James Longstreet who was not only his commander but an old acquaintance from the military academy. McLaws called Longstreet, "A humbug man of small capacity, very obstinate and not at all chivalrous, exceedingly conceited and totally selfish." It was no surprise that the two men had an argument and Longstreet brought several charges against his old friend following the failed Knoxville campaign. President Davis however sided with McLaws and Longstreet was the one to draw censure from the War Department. Still, it was McLaws who received a transfer.

He was particularly suited to defend against a siege outside Savannah because he had begun his Confederate career in that city and later earned a reputation in the Army of Northern Virginia for his defensive positioning. In Savannah, his good eye for terrain and defensive posture would bode well for battery placement in the perimeter line around the city. McLaws was such a sturdy defensive fighter that one of his

Sherman Takes Savannah

officers compared him to the Roman soldier who "stood his post in Herculaneum until the lava ran over him."

Gen. Ambrose "Rans" Wright had 2,700 men and 32 guns to protect the remaining seven miles of the line. His flank rested on the Little Ogeechee River where the Savannah and Gulf Railroad crossed. Wright's shaky force consisted of militia, local volunteers, and a few veterans.

Gen. Wright had replaced Hugh Mercer when Mercer had fallen to ill health. He was born near Augusta and settled there as an adult. Wright was a lawyer before the war and president of the Georgia senate. Wright began his service as a colonel with the 3rd Georgia Infantry and was promoted to brigadier general in June 1862. He had led a brigade under Robert E. Lee and although he was court-martialed for disobedience toward superior officers after Gettysburg, he handled his own defense and was acquitted. Temporarily, he returned to politics. In the autumn of 1863 he was elected to the Georgia State Senate and left the army until the legislature adjourned. He returned to active duty in the Virginia theatre. but a minor illness forced him home again in 1864. He and his brigade were part of the retreating southern force in the Seven Days battles and on through the entrenchment at Petersburg. He received a severe wound at Antietam and upon recovery was promoted to major general and ordered to Georgia. After Sherman had captured Milledgeville he assumed command of the state militia east of the Oconee River. He was promoted to major general and soon joined Hardee at Savannah. His contemporaries described him as to self-willed and combative with too much dash and not enough coolness.

* * * * * * * * * * * *

Sherman knew there was no way the city could defend 15 miles of perimeter against his army of 60,000, most of which

H. Ronald Freeman

were battle-tested soldiers. His troops continued to advance toward Savannah and McLaws in the center was only able at best to fight a delaying action barely slowing the Yankee columns. Meanwhile, temperatures dropped dramatically and soldiers in the trenches on both sides were subjected to freezing rains and the slush of cold swamp water. Rebel snipers were positioned so as to take advantage of any Yankees foolish enough to start fires.

Soldiers trooped through cold rains and struggled through bone chilling, shoulder-deep water. After wading through a swamp, one soldier wrote, "Our bones were fairly frozen and the marrow within them congealed." It was certainly a change from their operations around Atlanta during the summer, when heat prostration was often a more serious threat than rebel bullets.

Union infantrymen scooped out shallow pits in the chilly black mud near the rebel fortifications. Some managed to gather enough dry wood to kindle fires but soon realized it was not a wise move when Confederate gunners opened fire on the flames. Amid whizzing cannonballs and bullets, the Yankees hastily stamped out the embers. As the cold nights wore on, men danced up and down in order to stay warm. They could never find enough dry land to set up camp.

Rebel fire was not the only problem facing the Yankees in front of Savannah. Their stomachs were growling with hunger. "The question of our supplies begins to look threatened," Maj. Hitchcock noted. Many units had no provisions left, and hardtack was being peddled among the troops for a dollar a biscuit. Confederate pickets taunted their counterparts about the situation, yelling, "Hey Yank, don't you want some hard bread? Come over here and get something to eat."

The Union army had arrived just in time to capture an entire rice crop, and men subsisted on it for two weeks. "Our men are now living almost entirely on rice," wrote one officer, as there was no meat, crackers, coffee or sugar. Whereas

Sherman Takes Savannah

they had lived on the land for a couple hundred miles after leaving Atlanta, the coastal plain was less populated and edible crops, except for rice, were not as abundant. Even hardtack was now in scarce supply. On the rebel side the situation was much the same. Their diet was rice, sweet potatoes and crusty bread.

Neither side had adequate shelter against the freezing weather. Uniforms were rag-tag, hair and beards were long and unkempt and shoes were scarce on both sides. The telltale difference was in battle-hardened experience. Union troops had been in the campaigns of Chattanooga and Atlanta and were seasoned soldiers. They also outnumbered the rebels about 6 to 1. Southern troops were quite the opposite of their northern counterparts. For the most part, they weren't veterans. Many were the old, the young, the infirmed and disabled, freed prisoners, and even some foreigners who were P.O.W.'s who were impressed into Confederate service. They were not exactly crack troops as their commanders were all too aware. Orders had been given to fire on the foreigners if they turned against the rebels.

As feared, this came to pass. Commanders learned through camp scuttlebutt that in fact two companies of foreigners planned to go over to the Yankees in masse. The leaders were disarmed, court-martialed and summarily executed that evening. Two deserters along with five conspirators were also sentenced to the firing squad. Due to poor marksmanship, two men were only wounded and had to be dispatched with a bullet to the head. Afterwards, the foreign battalion was dissolved and many of its men sent back to prison.

H. Ronald Freeman

Battle Lines Drawn

Sherman knew he was in the catbird seat. He was busying himself with siege tactics and had requisitioned for the big guns to be brought in from Port Royal. His army of 60,000 continued to encircle the city closing in on Hardee's scanty army of 10,000.

Hardee was cornered, surrounded on three sides in addition to having the Union blockade to his rear off the coast. His only advantage was that any assault had to come along the main roads into town. These were heavily defended and he knew that Sherman was aware of this. Taking that approach would be costly to the Union in terms of casualties. In addition, Sherman was not sure of the strength of the rebel defenders. He speculated on Savannah's strength at 10,000 but certainly no more than 20,000, most of whom would not be veterans .He suspected about 10,000 but confirmation of that number hadn't been made.

The Union plan was to shell the city rather than mount an assault that would have forced them to use the few causeways through the marsh for access. Sherman was unwilling to risk losing any more lives than necessary.

The only escape for the Confederates was the Union Way, the plank road on the Carolina side of the Savannah River, and from there on through the swamps and to Hardeeville about 15 miles from Savannah. Sherman had not occupied that side of the River primarily due to the predominance of marsh and rice fields and knowing his troops would be bogged down. Gen. Slocum was not in agreement. He was in favor of immediately fortifying the opposite shore in force and totally closing Hardee in.

Hardee was not aware of Gen. Slocum's plan to cut off routes across the Savannah River and that could have changed his perspective. However, the Union generals were having a debate on whether they should send a division or maybe even a corps to bottle up the rebels. Sherman had

Sherman Takes Savannah

second thoughts. He was reticent to split his army since it might be needed later in Virginia and in that event have to be transferred by sea. Also, he was not eager to commit troops to the marshy terrain across the river.

After further deliberation, Sherman changed his mind about fortifying the Carolina side of the river. He somewhat relented and allowed five Union companies to be dispatched across the River from Argyle Island on December 15th but as night fell, they returned. Slocum pushed for more, even as much as the strength of a corps. Sherman was not convinced and decided to wait a few more days. Then, Gen. Slocum would cross the Savannah River and block any road leading out from the city on the South Carolina side. Once that was accomplished, Savannah would be sealed like a tomb.

The final decision was to send only a brigade. Here again, the brigade was not to block the escape route into South Carolina but to block a road on the Carolina side leading to Augusta. Sherman justified his decision by saying a pontoon crossing would be exposed to rebel gunboats and even if successful, the troops would then be isolated by the broad river.

What Sherman didn't know was that the fear of southern naval power was ludicrous. Neither the ironclads nor the *Isondiga*, the South's one gunboat could get that far upriver because of their deep draft. If made, the pontoon crossing would have had nothing to fear.

An entire brigade did cross on the 19th and drove the Confederates from an important position in a mill on the Izard Plantation on the Carolina side. But once there it was almost impossible to advance because Wheeler's cavalry had been dispatched to the Carolina shore and rebel artillery was defending Hardee's back door escape path. The area was in rice fields that the Confederates had flooded to a depth of eighteen inches. Bridges across the canals had been burned and artillery commanded the only approaches across narrow dikes.

H. Ronald Freeman

Probably behind Sherman's logic was also the communication from Gen. Grant requesting that Sherman consider embarking his army by sea to join him in Virginia to hasten the defeat of Robert E. Lee. Sherman wanted to keep his army together in the event that did come about.

But another factor was heavy on Sherman's mind as well. Earlier in the war the Union army had been defeated at Ball's Bluff along the Potomac River. Union commanders had split their forces to occupy both sides of the river and had paid a heavy price for their mistake. Sherman was very conscious of that error and didn't want to duplicate it by dividing his army between two sides of a deep river that was still controlled by Confederate gunboats.

Sherman considered his options. He could either assault the town or starve the occupants out on a protracted siege. Assault was given the nod and his men began preparations and constructing rafts, ladders and footbridges. The attack was scheduled for the 21st. Halfway through the preparations, he changed his mind - again. Attack meant casualties and he was unwilling to put his men in harm's way when there may be a bloodless means of capturing the town and maybe the rebel army too.

There was still another option and Sherman went to Hilton Head to meet with Gen. Foster. He wanted to strategize about how to close the back door to Hardee. His plan involved Col. Hatch's division that had been attempting to sever the rail line at Pocotaligo some 30 miles north of Savannah. They could move down and seal the casket on Hardee.

* * * * * * * * * * * * * * * * * * * *

In anticipation, in late November, Gen. Hardee had shifted his heavy guns from the river approaches to the western edge of the city, and then put every man in Savannah to work preparing fortifications. Hardee did not care whether his new militiamen were active, furloughed, able or not. All

Sherman Takes Savannah

were organized into military units under Gen. Lafayette McLaws, who had retreated into the city from outlying areas.

To prevent a naval attack on the city, the Savannah River was obstructed by a double row of cribs placed in the water at the northern edge of Elba Island. The cribs consisted of timbers twenty-inches in girth, securely bound and filled with bricks and cobblestones from Savannah's city streets. The cribs were a height of thirty-five feet and extended across both channels of the river.

The primary defenses of the town ran in an arc from the Savannah River on the west around and back to the river on the east. It was not a perfect semi-circle but varied according to topography. It snaked in and out from three to nine miles depending on terrain.

The cannon were huge 24 to 32 pound siege guns removed from the coastal batteries. In addition, Hardee had eleven batteries totaling 48 field artillery pieces that he could place at any threatened point in the line. That was the good news, for he certainly had no reserve troops available to stem Union breakthroughs. The Confederates were outnumbered 60,000 to 10,000, six to one, but at least their opponents did not outgun them.

Confederate troops used a network of creeks that fed the rivers and situated their positions behind the impenetrable swampy streams. Once in place, they flooded the surrounding area to a depth of three to six feet by cutting through the rice dikes and opening sluice gates.

As stated, there were actually only five avenues into the city and they were rail beds and roads built on narrow causeways. They were also the points of obvious defense by the rebels and usually their heaviest guns were positioned there. A complex of large batteries equipped with the heavy guns blocked the narrow causeways that led through the swamps, canals, and flooded rice fields into the historic city. Those causeways were used by the Central Railroad, Gulf

H. Ronald Freeman

Railroad, and roads leading to Augusta, Louisville, and south to the Ogeechee River. They were the only practical means of access.

Some of the gun emplacements were placed forward of the main line, giving the Confederate gunners a devastating enfilading fire against any Federal attack. Where permitted by the swampy terrain, infantry trenches and rifle pits connected the positions, and lines of sharpened logs occupied every inch of firm ground behind the water barriers.

Union sentries near the Savannah River spotted the smoke of three steamers rapidly approaching their position from upstream toward Augusta. The battery was quickly readied to prevent the Confederates from reaching Savannah. At 2,500 yards the Yankees opened fire on the side-wheel gunboats *Macon, Sampson* and the unarmed *Resolute.* The gunboats, in line behind the *Resolute*, returned fire with heavy guns, but already the Federals had struck the lead boat several times at half-mile range. As they rounded a bend, exposing them to a raking shore fire from the Union battery the gunboats got up steam and turned back. In the confusion they rammed the *Resolute,* which then drifted helplessly and ran aground on Argyle Island in mid-river.

Her crew lowered small boats and was about to escape when Union infantry appeared and fired a volley, wounding one man. The *Resolute* complement of seven officers and twenty-two men, plus considerable provisions, was captured and taken to the Georgia shore.

Union soldiers had formed a line around the Confederate defense in the shape of an irregular crescent as a companion to the Confederate arc. The 14th and 20th Corps of Slocum's left wing faced the Confederates from the Savannah River to the Ogeechee Canal. The 15th and 17th of Howard's right wing faced the Rebels from the canal to the Little Ogeechee River. The Federals were so close to Savannah they could hear the church bells ringing.

Sherman Takes Savannah

After the Union guns were moved into place, they began their pounding of the Confederate line as they attempted to determine its points of strength and weakness. Gen. Hardee, overall commander of Savannah, was understandably nervous. On December 8th an alarmed Gen. Beauregard asked Hardee to come to Charleston for a conference. Believing the situation in Savannah was too desperate for him to leave, Hardee requested that Beauregard come to him. Beauregard met with Hardee on December 9th as Sherman enveloped the city.

Beauregard did not believe the reports on Sherman's strength at nearly 60,000. His own intelligence surmised Union troop strength at closer to 20,000 and he had reports that they were loading onto the boats off the coast to retreat back to the North. Kilpatrick had so effectively screened Sherman's advance that Hardee could obtain little accurate information about Union movements.

Gen. Pierre Gustave Bureaugard

Hardee explained his plans to evacuate the city by boat, if it became necessary, but Beauregard believed a boatlift would be unable to move the equipment necessary for the troops. After his assessment he ordered a series of pontoon bridges to be laid across the Savannah River to South Carolina in the event an evacuation became necessary. He reminded Hardee again not to let his men be trapped.

Ultimately the decision to fight or flee was Hardee's; hold the city as long as advisable but in all cases to preserve the garrison for deployment in operations elsewhere. Hardee knew that without reinforcements he was compelled to evacuate. When the time came, he planned for his army to leave the city via the pontoon bridges laid across the Savannah River to South Carolina.

In order to reach the Carolina shore the bridges would have to cross three separate bodies of water, all substantial streams. There would actually be three bridges. The first would originate from Savannah at the foot of West Broad Street (now Martin Luther King, Jr. Boulevard) and initially cross the main channel to Hutchinson Island. The second span would connect Hutchinson Island with Pennyworth Island and the final leg would be across the Back River to the marshes of Carolina.

The bridge and evacuation was the final option. Thousands of laborers, including slaves, federal prisoners, rebel troops and civilians began the task of bridging the great river. Hardee's engineers used their ingenuity to assemble all available materials to be used in the construction. From both sides of the river, engineers collected boats and rice flats. These were actually shallow barges, 70 to 85 feet long, lashed together with chains and ropes to act as pontoons. They were floated into place with the tide and held in place by makeshift anchors using the wheels from rail cars that had been stripped. On top of the flats were heavy timbers from the city's docks that had been virtually stripped of wood. The time in which it was erected reflected to the credit of those in charge. Many observers felt it was truly astonishing.

Like all construction projects, there were delays and also some vandalism. This time from their own side when Wheeler's cavalry mistook some of the critical rice flats as belonging to the federals and destroyed them.

Sherman Takes Savannah

It was not a pretty sight and was described as a shaggy undulating monster with floats of all sizes and shapes covered with timbers at crazy angles. Hopefully it was structurally sound. Even so it still left the problem of the marshy, muddy surface of the two islands to cross. They had to be shorn up in spots where the ground was soft and artillery caissons and supply wagons could bog down. In these areas it was required that plank roads be laid as hastily as possible. To offset that hurdle, men, mules and wagons crept across the soft surface to dump tons of rice straw along with logs and planks until they had created a crude road that would bear the weight of the army's loaded wagons.

Fortunately for the rebels, the work was being completed well within their lines and out of sight of any inquisitive Yankees. Unfortunately, the weather turned cold and rainy rendering conditions for construction challenging at best.

The escape plan involved stealth. To avoid being overrun, the Confederates needed to slip out in the dark of night. This brought up the question of noise suppression since troops, wagons and artillery even crossing at night could be a loud undertaking. To this end both rice and straw were scattered on the bridge decking.

The only positive thing was that it was being done out of sight of the federal army. Beauregard returned to Savannah on the 16th and was alarmed the bridges were only about a third complete. He was livid. Everyone available was then assigned to the project: sailors, militia and about a thousand slaves.

While Beauregard was in town, he along with Hardee devised a specific plan for actual evacuation of the Confederate army. Finally, having thrown all available men and resources into the fray, the pontoon bridges were ready. To Beauregard's credit, his wrath had worked wonders and on the 19th, the bridges were complete.

H. Ronald Freeman

Exodus

It was now December 17th and Gen. Hardee was in receipt of a surrender demand written personally by Sherman. It was delivered by Sherman's brother-in-law, Col. Charles Ewing who arrived under a white flag of truce. The guns on the battlefield had become silent from both sides. The communication had been taken directly to Hardee. He and Gen. Beauregard, who had arrived the night before, reviewed Sherman's demand.

Sherman pointed out that he controlled the Ogeechee River and was now being amply supplied by the blockading boats offshore. He also controlled every means of access into the city. Heavy guns had been brought up that were capable of sending shot into the heart of the city. If Hardee would capitulate, liberal terms would be granted to both the troops and the inhabitants of the city. Otherwise, he would be forced to resort to assault or starvation. In either case he wouldn't restrain his army from taking revenge against Savannah and other southern cities that had acted so prominently in dragging the country into a civil war. He would wait a reasonable time for response before opening up with his heavy guns.

It only took a short time for Hardee to respond. He pointed out that Sherman's closest forces were still four miles out from the city and at that distance they were too far to hurl destructive shot and reach the town. He took exception to the statement that the federals controlled all arteries into the city since he was in constant communication with his superiors. Hardee also addressed Sherman's implied threat of releasing his army to avenge the North against large cities like Savannah. He let him know that he had always conducted his campaigns in accordance with the strict rules of civilized warfare and would regret Sherman not doing the same. If that became the case it may force him to also forget the rules in the future. In short, the demand for surrender was refused.

Sherman Takes Savannah

After Hardee's reply, Sherman immediately ordered preparations for attack. They planned to hit the line at every point accessible on the long perimeter. All was ready, but once again, the general had second thoughts. To his credit he was reluctant to sacrifice any of his men in a frontal assault. While he knew his troops could overcome the weak Confederate perimeter, he had no wish to lose any troops by means of a direct attack. Savannah's fate was sealed and forfeiting life needlessly would be criminal. Sherman's reputation was one of conserving lives and this was a good example. Rather than a frontal assault, he would flush the rebs from the brush.

Citizens of Savannah had heard the stories of what Union troops were doing to the people of Georgia as they burned a scar through the state on their way to Savannah. Pillage, looting, rape and murder were the reports and the female population of the town took special heed. It was with a distinctive dread they awaited the coming of Sherman's northern horde closing in on them like a plague.

From Charleston, Beauregard ordered the evacuation as quickly and expeditiously as possible. Hardee in turn met with his commanders and prepared a timeline of when each unit would withdraw and head for the river. The pullout would commence after sundown on the evening of the 20th. At dark, the field batteries were to withdraw from their positions as quietly as possible and begin their crossing on the pontoon bridge.

Even before the defending Confederates were organized to retreat, evacuating civilians put the newly completed bridges to the test. There was a steady stream of wagons, carriages and foot traffic crossing the river to seek the safety of the other side.

Scheduled time of departure for the troops was 8:00 p.m. The first units to cross would be the artillery and to this end the wheels of caissons and wagons would be muffled with blankets and rope. McLaws would follow and Smith would fall

H. Ronald Freeman

in behind him. Troops manning the batteries several miles downriver would spike their guns and meet the transport boats at Ft. Jackson. From there they would cross the river and meet up with the main column at Screven's Ferry, where the bridge ended on the Carolina side. A heavy shelling of Union lines, launched at sundown just before the pullout, would hopefully cover the withdrawal. This would also serve to expend ammunition that otherwise would fall into enemy hands.

After the shelling, guns facing the enemy would be quietly disabled and excess ammunition disposed of by sinking it in the river so as to not make a suspicious noise. Silence was the watchword.

On the western front, facing the enemy, the Confederates abandoned their posts on schedule throughout the night while making certain their fires continued to burn. There was a curtain of gloom and despondency as the men retreated silently from their positions to the foot of the street to the bridge. Once there they joined with others in the steady tramping as the proud rebel army slinked out of town and into the safety of Carolina. The wounded and infirmed had to be left behind.

Sherman Takes Savannah

Evacuation

Throughout the night of December 20th, in the shadows of the spires of Savannah, a long column of cannon, men, and wagons waited on West Broad Street (MLK Blvd.) for their turn to cross the bridge. Fog rolled in, making the journey across the creaking, swaying spans seem like a terrifying nightmare; infantry stomped, wagons creaked, teamsters cursed and mules brayed in fear.

The retreat was not without mishap as an occasional wagon and its team would become unstable and swerve off the bridge into the black swirling water, never to be seen again. There was only quiet acceptance from the onlookers. No expression, no sympathy, just acceptance and a continuation of forward progress.

"The constant tread of the troops and the rumbling of the caissons and wagons as they poured over those long floating bridges was a sad sound," wrote one soldier, "and by the glare of the light from fires at the base of the bridge it seemed like an immense funeral procession somber in its ritual of leaving the city in the dead of night."

As planned with the big guns, shells were expended and then the cannon were spiked. Anything usable was thrown into the canals and swamps and artillery ammunition in the river. As the river batteries were abandoned, men

H. Ronald Freeman

chopped up the gun carriages and destroyed their rammers and sponges.

It was a dark night where everything seemed to move according to some unwritten but preordained pattern. Men, horses and wagons trudged onward in what seemed to observers as an endless mass of motion.

As the Confederate wagons rumbled toward Carolina across the river, the gun emplacements continued booming to hide the noise of the retreat. Some described the trek across the pontoon bridge as a rhythmic clanking from an army in retreat.

When they reached the Carolina side of the river, the army units planned to converge on Hardeeville, about 15 miles from Savannah. Then it would split, each command with its own orders. Gen. Gustavus Smith would proceed to Charleston by train on the Charleston & Savannah Railroad. Gen. McLaws would hold a defensive position along the Combahee River and the others would head for James Island near the coast of Charleston. Wheeler's cavalry was charged with holding off enemy interference of the retreat.

Once across the river the hardships had just begun. It was still a good march to Hardeeville and some of the men had little left but their blankets. As they trudged north they could hear the explosions of the Confederate gunships as they were being destroyed.

The Georgia fleet in Savannah was given orders to attempt to escape or, for those still under construction, be destroyed. The *CSS Savannah* would cover the retreat and then attempt to steam to Charleston. The gunboats, if their drafts would permit, would punch through enemy lines and reach Augusta. Otherwise, they would try for the Atlantic via the Wilmington River. Secretary of the Confederate Navy Stephen Mallory was adamant that the boats make a fight of it. He even countermanded Beauregard's orders and said if the boats are to go down they must do so in combat while engaging the enemy. He felt it important to the cause that they

Sherman Takes Savannah

not be destroyed by their own side but to go out with dignity. It ended up being a moot point since his order arrived after the evacuation.

The naval evacuation was an illustration of Murphy's Law. The things that can possibly go wrong becoming the reality. The smaller boats, because of their deep drafts, were unable to get upstream as hoped and were torched. During the evening, the *Georgia's* guns were spiked, and she was scuttled at her moorings. When sailors opened her seacocks, the *Georgia* sank like the rock she was, so quickly that many men were forced to scramble for safety without their belongings. The *Georgia* had never fired her guns in anger.

The ironclad *Milledgeville*, recently launched but as yet not completed, was burned to the waterline and sank in mid-river. After their ceaseless labor, it deeply hurt her builders to torch the ship, which had been expected to be the most powerful ironclad produced in Savannah. Commodore Tattnall viewed the destruction of his navy with grim resignation and then joined Gen. Hardee and his troops in the Hardeeville bound column.

Early on the morning of the 21st, the navy yard with a number of vessels under construction and two steamboats, the *Isondiga* and *Firefly*, were put to the torch. The last troops to cross the bridge were cast as silhouettes by the flames. Around the scuttled boats were pieces of the dismantled pontoon bridge that had been severed from the Savannah side when the last of the troops had crossed.

Hardee's troops were still streaming over the bridges when the first of the looting broke out in the city. When order and the threat of prosecution left, lawlessness entered. It was an old pattern. The scum of the city, seeing their opportunity for ill-gotten gains, started smashing the doors of shops and carting off the available goods.

At dawn, the federals began to sense the stillness from the opposing lines. Cautiously they began to creep forward.

H. Ronald Freeman

As they approached the rebel defenses, they saw the still smoldering campfires but no enemy except for a few wounded.

* * * * * * * * * * *

Hardee's proud but exhausted army trickled into Hardeeville on December 21st. The day was extremely cold and the early arrivals had to crack the thick ice that had formed in the railroad water tanks to supply the locomotives that had been waiting for the troops. It was important to Hardee that the trains be ready when he was.

Some of the men in Hardee's ragtag army were volunteers that had been impressed into service when the call went out to stop Sherman's advance. Many of these were Savannah citizens but others were from Macon and Augusta who worked in those town's factories supplying war goods. Those men were released from further service.

The immediate strategy was to leave from Hardeeville and set up a defense behind the Combahee River. The 49 pieces of light artillery brought with them from Savannah would aid in this defense.

Hardee was satisfied with his exploit and for many years he would recount what he felt was one of the gr

Cotton on the Wharf

Sherman Takes Savannah

strategic maneuvers of his career. He had lost the city but had salvaged 10,000 southern troops to march north and join up with Gen. Johnston. They would substantially bolster the strength of the Confederate forces that would be aligned as Sherman moved to unite with Grant.

Beauregard's aide agreed with Hardee saying, "This was one of the neatest achievements of the war." But not everyone was singing praises for Hardee. The Confederate Congress wanted to know why he would leave such a valuable quantity of cotton intact for Sherman to come in and just take it. Why not at least destroy the cotton and keep it out of Union hands. It didn't add to his defense that his brother Andrew was a cotton merchant in Savannah and could find a way to profit from the cotton left behind.

With patience Hardee explained that the cotton was not all conveniently in one place where it could be destroyed. It was all over the town and manpower was in short supply to bring it to a central point. Savannah's cotton yield, worth a fortune to the hungry factories of the world, was distributed among cellars and warehouses throughout the city.

When President Davis and the Confederate Congress demanded to know why it had not been destroyed or removed, Hardee explained that the railroads had been needed for military purposes and men were not available to gather it for burning. Such an act, he continued, might have destroyed the city and would certainly have tipped his hand. The primary reason for not destroying the cotton was that he was trying to save his army. In that regard all men and wagons were needed to supply his lines and construct a bridge across the river rather than hauling cotton. The federal government later sold the cotton for thirty million dollars.

H. Ronald Freeman

Surrender

As Hardee and his troops were evacuating, Savannah's mayor, Dr. Richard Arnold, and members of the city council were in session. Meeting in their chamber at the City Exchange (City Hall) building, they even called in several of the town's prominent citizens to express their concerns and get their input. It was a time of decision and the choice was not hard. They knew with the army gone, their only course of action was to surrender the city. What else could they do? Savannah was now Sherman's for the taking and in only a few hours, the Yankees would be among them.

On the morning of December 21st as the remnants of Hardee's retreating army was still crossing the river, Mayor Arnold and the aldermen started out the Augusta Road (Louisville Road) to meet the Union army and formally surrender the city. Rather than waiting for the Yankees to come to them, it seemed to be a better course of action to go out to the approaching invaders.

But even this presented a special problem. Although they had made prior arrangements for transportation, the retreating Confederate army needed the horses they reserved and there was only one buggy left for everyone.

Somehow the party got separated and a Union sentry intercepted two of the aldermen on foot. They were taken to Gen. Geary who without ceremony accepted the surrender of the city from the sheepish aldermen. It was only a short time later that Mayor Arnold was brought in and then formally surrendered the town to the Union army. They were unaware that Gen. Sherman was in Hilton Head conferring with others on strategy and not in Savannah for the surrender. Arnold requested Union protection for the lives and private property of the city inhabitants. Geary agreed and assured the mayor that any offense by his troops would be punishable by death.

The mayor escorted one of Geary's brigades commanded by Col. Henry A. Barnum into the city. They

Sherman Takes Savannah

entered by the way of Augusta Road to West Broad Street (M.L.K. Blvd.) and then north to Bay Street and east to the City Exchange. It was six a.m. on the morning of the 21st. The Yankees were now in official possession of the city. For the escaping Confederates, the timing was close. As the federals were advancing down West Broad the Confederate engineers, who were severing the Savannah side of the bridge from its moorings, observed them coming. As the current swept the loosened side of the rickety bridge downstream, the engineers dashed back across to the Carolina side as quickly as possible.

Even with the influx of new troops, albeit of a different stripe, looting and lawlessness continued. It was something

CSS Savannah Explodes

that would not stop of its own accord. To address the problem, Geary immediately placed the city under marshal law and began patrols of the streets on a regular basis. The Savannah newspaper, *The Republican*, acknowledged federal control and

H. Ronald Freeman

asked all citizens to remain within the safety of their homes until a formal system of law was enacted to protect life and property.

All members of the Confederate military had not left. Stragglers including ironclad *Savannah* continued to ply the waters of the river. It was Beauregard's intention that the *Savannah* make for the open waters of the Atlantic and if necessary engage the Union fleet. It was not to be. Confederate torpedoes, submerged in the water of the Savannah and Wilmington Rivers to keep Union boats out, were also very effective at keeping Confederate boats in.

Necessary equipment for removing the mines was not available. This left the *Savannah's* commander, Capt. Thomas W. Brent but two choices. He could surrender a valuable ironclad to the enemy who could certainly find a way to get it to deeper water. Or, he could abandon and explode the pride of the South and keep it out of Federal hands. Good southerner that he was, he chose the latter.

About 7:30 that evening the crew abandoned ship after placing kegs of black powder aboard. Strategically, the captain set fire to the ironclad. In small boats, he and his men rowed for the Carolina shore and set out to rejoin Hardee. Later that evening, they and everyone else for miles around heard it. At about 11:30 the boat exploded and was engulfed in flames, emitting enough light to be seen from an eight-mile distance. The skies were ablaze and the explosion was horrendous. The *CSS Savannah,* like most of her sister ships, was no more.

In retrospect it was just as well. There were two Union ironclads waiting just offshore for the southern gunboat. Earlier in the day Gen. Geary had dispatched a 400-man force to occupy Ft. Jackson downriver and when U.S. colors were raised, the *Savannah* responded with cannon fire. As it turned out it was the only pleasure the *Savannah* had. It would be the one time the small fort, built for the War of 1812, would ever receive hostile fire.

Sherman Takes Savannah

Since Gen. Geary's division of the 20th Corps was the first to enter the city, he had been formally appointed as the city's military commander. The choice for the city was fortunate indeed. This tall black-bearded general was a friendly man who had a genius for getting along with people. He also had experience in government which was combined with a strong sense of humanity. Most of the difficult situations he encountered were handled with diplomacy and tact. Within a short period even the Yankee haters had to concede, he was doing an excellent job.

The Yankees were ecstatic. They had Savannah and all it had to offer. They again had food and it had all been acquired with little hardship and only a token sacrifice of life. In the 37 days since leaving Atlanta only ten officers and 93 men had been killed. Twenty-four officers and 404 men were wounded with one officer and 277 men missing. Many others were forced to join, at least temporarily, into Confederate service.

On the Southern side, 77 officers had been captured by the federals. Sherman's aide-de-camp, Maj. George W. Nichols said, "We have won a magnificent prize." An additional 1,200 rebels, mostly sick and wounded, who could not be transported, were taken in Savannah. Some captive Confederates were deserters, but others were "galvanized Yankees," or Union soldiers captured and then threatened with death if they did not join the southern army. In one night 27 of these "converted Confederates" deserted to Gen. Slocum near Savannah.

Gen. Howard reported freeing 3,500 slaves during his march, which seems a conservative estimate. Perhaps they were included with those who persevered and stayed with the Union army as camp followers until they reached Savannah. Gen. Slocum claimed 14 thousand slaves trailed along with his army of the left wing. The best estimates are that 25 thousand slaves joined the column at some point and six thousand were still remaining when they reached Savannah.

H. Ronald Freeman

In Georgia, Sherman's men stole 6,900 horses and mules and over 20 thousand head of cattle. They appropriated over ten million pounds of corn and an equal amount of fodder. The number of consumed or merely slaughtered hogs, chickens, turkeys, amounts of corn, sweet potatoes, other vegetables and fruits, was incalculable. One soldier estimated that 100 thousand hogs were killed on the march. Howard's medical director found the men's health "peculiarly gratifying." He attributed it to an abundance of nutritious food, and particularly of vegetables.

Gen. Slocum's army destroyed 7,000 bales of cotton; Howard's, 3,500. An additional 35 thousand bales, more than originally thought, were captured in Savannah. The city also yielded 209 cannon, most of them heavy siege guns, 2,300 rifles, and 6,500 bladed weapons. Among the cannon was a brass six-pounder bearing the State of Georgia coat of arms and engraved with the words *Georgia Military Institute.* Poe, Sherman's engineer, suggested sending it to West Point.

Additionally, the Confederates abandoned 27 thousand rounds of artillery ammunition and 51 thousand infantry rounds. Left in the city were 13 locomotives, 190 rail cars, and three steamboats. Sherman was delighted to report in the capture of Savannah, "a perfect string of forts," and a population of 22 thousand people returned to the Union.

It was estimated that Sherman's soldiers had inflicted over one billion dollars worth of damage on Georgia. Twenty million dollars worth had benefited the army and the rest was pure waste.

Sherman was not present for his army's grand entrance into the city. He was on Hilton Head Island conferring with other generals. He was delayed in his return to Georgia when his vessel ran aground during a storm. The general had not heard that Hardee had evacuated Savannah until a tug arrived to pull the boat out of the mud bank left by the low tide. He took it in stride knowing his victory was substantial and gained without loss of life. That was his primary concern. On that morning he finally rode into the city. Since he had spent time in

Sherman Takes Savannah

Savannah a number of years before, it was like a homecoming for him.

Riding down Bull Street toward the river, he viewed the aristocratic houses. At the Custom House on Bay Street he dismounted and ascended to the roof to get a better prospect of the city. It now lay literally at his feet. There he surveyed it all; the rice fields on the Carolina side, the city to the south and the smoldering wreck of the *CSS Savannah* still afloat. The river was just below him and he noted where Hardee escaped through the only door left. "I knocked daylight through Georgia," Sherman told a friend and no one could dispute his claim.

Many though, would second-guess Sherman even after the war. They felt his most important business was containing Hardee and not going to Hilton Head to plot future strategy. He should have occupied the Carolina shore in force with a body of troops and then he could easily have overpowered the sparse Confederate line and tightened the noose on Hardee. Even Secretary of War Stanton wrote to Grant of his disappointment in Sherman for letting Hardee escape. He felt they were protracting the war.

Others felt it was Sherman's intention for Hardee to escape. This made a fight unnecessary and spared many lives. It was this attitude that caused him anguish at the thought of sailing his troops to Virginia. Fighting against Lee meant killing whereas a march through the Carolinas meant further breaking of the Confederate will at the cost of only a few fatalities. Psychological warfare made sense and traditional warfare did not. Carnage had solved little in the past three years. What he really wanted was to open the Savannah River to Union traffic and this is what he accomplished.

H. Ronald Freeman

The Pulaski House

Sherman's earlier time in Savannah was as a young lieutenant and he had been quartered in the Pulaski House on Johnson Square. This is where he and his staff again visited in their search for lodging. He asked his officers to search for more suitable quarters where they could find a stable for their horses.

While waiting at the Pulaski House many visitors including Mayor Arnold and Gen. Hardee's brother Noble, who was a cotton broker, called on him. He was also visited by Charles Green, a British subject and another cotton broker in the city. Mr. Green offered his handsome and well-appointed house to the general for his headquarters while he was in the city.

At first Sherman was reluctant to accept. He preferred using public buildings like governor's mansions and the residences of other officials. Green was adamant and insisted. Sherman looked over his house and discovered it to be just what he needed. He stipulated however, that he and his staff would provide their own meals.

Sherman Takes Savannah

Green Mansion

Green turned over to Sherman his entire house with the exception of a few rooms above the dining area for his own use. Sherman personally selected a bedroom on the second floor at the southwest corner. In a letter to his wife he jested that he occupied a magnificent mansion and was living like a gentleman. Because the Green house belonged to a foreigner, the U.S. Government paid him a token rent. Of course as soon as other residents realized the advantage and safety of foreign citizenship, foreign flags began appearing over many buildings.

Actually, Green had a vested interest in all the cotton left on the wharves and elsewhere, and many felt his overture was to protect his property. His rebuttal to the accusation was that he didn't want others to submit to the embarrassment of having their home commandeered into service by the Union. Whatever his ulterior motives, he did not recover his cotton.

H. Ronald Freeman

Sherman accepted his offer, finding Green to be extremely pleasant and courteous.

One of the first callers on Sherman was A. G. Browne, an agent of the U.S. Treasury, who had come to claim the confiscated cotton for the government. While there he suggested Sherman send a telegram to President Lincoln presenting Savannah as a Christmas gift. Sherman loved the idea and readily agreed. Lincoln received the telegram on Christmas Eve and released it to newspapers throughout the northern states.

Savannah Ga.
Dec 22. 1864

To his Excellency,
President Lincoln.

Dear Sir,

"I beg to present you as a Christmas Gift, the City of Savannah with 150 heavy guns and plenty of ammunition; and also about 25,000 bales of Cotton."

W. T. Sherman
Maj. Genl.

Lincoln responded, "Many, many thanks for your Christmas gift, the capture of Savannah. But what next? I suppose it will be safe if I leave it to Gen. Grant and yourself to decide"

Citizens of Savannah were obviously wondering what was going on now that they were occupied and how they would be affected. They petitioned Mayor Arnold for a public meeting

Sherman Takes Savannah

that was held the night of December 28th. The mood was one of defeat. As a body they voted to put an end to hostility and again submit to the U.S. Constitution. For Savannah, the war was over. It was hard to say what the deciding factor was. It may have been that seeing the Yankees up close and personal, they observed that they weren't the ogres they had been painted.

The effects and ravages of war were noticeable everywhere, business was almost entirely suspended, and nearly every store was closed. The houses were also carefully closed and very few residents were to be seen. Fences were broken down, sidewalks and wharves were going to ruin, and dead horses and mules were lying about the streets by the dozens.

Seeing the remorse of the town, Sherman showed his and ordered the food supplies left by the fleeing Confederate army to be turned over to the local citizens. But foods aside, there were many other shortages in Savannah in January 1865. Coal, necessary not only for heating but also for cooking, was almost non-existent. This meant that whatever was available and flammable was burned.

Sherman issued Field Order No. 143. It stated that the citizens must decide whether they would remain in Savannah and accept the occupation, or be evacuated. Only two hundred people volunteered to leave the now Union held city.

Cannon from captured Ft. McAllister, the river forts, and the city's fortifications that were not needed for Savannah's defense were dismounted and shipped to Ft. Pulaski and Hilton Head. They felt there was still a possibility of counterattack.

Sherman ordered the torpedoes in the Savannah River removed, and sent crews to dismantle the crib obstructions. Islands of mud that had formed around the cribs had to be dredged before the stout cribs and their brick and cobblestone contents could be removed. The mines left submerged in the

H. Ronald Freeman

rivers were being cleared. Only then would it be possible to supply his army fully. The war machine the Confederate's left behind was being dismantled.

Shortly after occupying Savannah, Sherman received word that he would not be required to go by ship to Virginia. "Your confidence in being able to march up and join this army pleases me," Grant wrote Sherman, "and I believe it can be done. The effect of such a campaign will be to disorganize and prevent the organization of new armies from their broken fragments. Without waiting further directions, you may make preparations to start on your northern expedition without delay. Break up the railroads in the Carolinas, and join the armies operating near Richmond as soon as you can."

Sherman responded, "The truth is the whole army is burning with an insatiable desire to wreak vengeance upon South Carolina, I almost tremble at its fate, but feel that she deserves all that seems in store for her. Many a person in Georgia has asked me why we did not go to South Carolina. When I answered I was en route for that state the invariable reply was, 'Well, if you will make those people feel the severities of war, we will pardon you for your devastation of Georgia.'" Apparently there was a weariness of war and a search to establish blame for the suffering they were feeling.

Sherman was indeed riding high and was also quoted as saying, "The President, the army, and even the world, ask me to strike hard and decisive blows.... I have cut the South in twain and have planned and executed a campaign that will be famous among the grand deeds of the world. I have been able to do it for really it was easy. But like one who has walked a narrow road back and wonders if he really did it, I have the evidence at hand. I am in a proud city with an elegant mansion at my command, surrounded by a brave and victorious army that looks to me as its head. Freed slaves flock to me and gaze at me as some wonderful being, and letters from my men pour in with words of flattery and praise. "

Sherman Takes Savannah

40 Acres and a Mule

Now that Savannah was again controlled by the federals, Washington couldn't wait to exert its influence and meddling. Sherman had done his job but it was only a military victory. Now it was time to make room for the meddlers and politicians.

As Sherman's army had cut a swath across the state, burning buildings and fields and freeing slaves as they went, camp followers more and more overwhelmed them. The liberated blacks didn't know where to go or what to do so they attached themselves to their chosen messiah. It became a problem for his advancing army as it neared Savannah since the roads were clogged with former slaves. Sherman reminded his commanders that they should keep in mind the question of supplies and it was their first duty to see to their men that bore arms. Clearly, freed slaves added an often unwanted burden on the quartermasters.

Gen. Jefferson Davis

Gen. Jefferson C. Davis of Indiana commanded Sherman's 14th Corps under Slocum. As they neared Springfield on December 3rd, they were unable to cross Ebenezer Creek since the retreating rebels had burned the bridge. Davis' unit worked through the night to replace the burned facility with a pontoon bridge and was ready to cross the ext morning. They were not alone. The entire black contingent that had been following them for days was also there. Davis had his men hold them at bay while his corps crossed and then to cut the bridge and pull it to the opposite bank. This left about five hundred camp followers, mostly women and children, on the other side.

When the blacks realized they were being left behind they panicked. Many rushed into the water and were swept away by the current and drowned. It was a terrible day. Davis came under harsh criticism even from his own men. It was described as a barbarous act but it wouldn't rest there. Northern newspapers picked up the story and even accused Wheeler's Confederate cavalry, that arrived after the incident was over, of killing many of the slaves. The story was totally untrue.

Sherman's combined army attracted thousands of black camp-followers as he swept from Atlanta to the sea. Even in this situation, much beyond his control, he came under criticism from northern liberals. Why didn't he pick up thousands more? They were available. Actually, many of the blacks returned to their homes after a few days of trailing the army not knowing what to do with their new freedom.

Liberal voices in Washington had gotten the ear of Lincoln and were letting him know that Sherman had an innate dislike for the blacks and drove them from his camps, did everything possible to keep them from tagging behind him and even allowed Wheeler's cavalry to massacre many at Ebenezer Creek. Sherman's retort and defense was that it was simply not true. He defended Davis' actions saying he wanted to save his bridge for future use, not that he wanted to cut off the blacks. He also set the story straight about Wheeler saying no one was killed at Ebenezer by the southern commander's cavalry.

Tongues were wagging on both sides about how Sherman was improperly handling the newly freed slaves. Almost as if he was seeking penance, Sherman turned attention to the more immediate problem of what to do with the blacks that had mobbed into Savannah behind his troops as they entered the city. He acted as a buffer between the blacks

Sherman Takes Savannah

and the northern recruiters who also flocked to the city. These vermin herded hundreds of ignorant victims into lockups until they agreed to enter the army where they were sold as substitutes for well-to-do draftees in the North. It was slave trade northern style, practiced by the invading carpetbaggers only focused on profit. Sherman told the blacks they were free and could not be forced into the army and he threatened the recruiters with arrest and jail time.

Edwin M. Stanton

Washington, however, wasn't buying Sherman's version of his officers' treatment of the blacks and on January 11th, Secretary of War Edwin M. Stanton arrived in Savannah on a surprise visit.

His primary purpose was to specifically meet with Sherman to get at what he believed to be the truth. Stanton, although a Democrat, was a strong abolitionist. The other purpose of his visit was to determine which governmental agency had the proper claim to the captured cotton valued at $25 million.

Stanton ruled there was no valid claim on the cotton except for the Treasury and ordered it shipped north and sold by the government. Claims from British brokers that the cotton had been purchased for export and rightfully belonged to them were rejected. Sherman commented, "Our soldiers throughout the war have been killed by British guns firing British ammunition and it was all were bought with rebel cotton."

In his meeting with Sherman, Stanton was blunt. Was Gen. Davis hostile in his feelings toward the blacks? Sherman

H. Ronald Freeman

assured him he was not. When the question of Ebenezer Creek arose, Davis was summoned to defend himself. In doing so he acknowledged there was loss of life by drowning at Ebenezer but he had received no stories of slaves being murdered by Wheeler's mounted troops. The explanation was accepted.

Sherman's mind was on fighting a war and not monitoring a change in the social order of the South. After all, he was a military man under orders. But even Sherman was not immune to the pervasive Black Republicanism of the day. Secretary of War Stanton had come to Savannah personally to observe the performance of the military versus the newly freed black population. He interviewed 20 black clergymen over several hours and personally recorded their answers to his question of, "What do you want for your own people?"

The meeting was held on the second floor of the Green mansion in Sherman's headquarters. The spokesman for the group was 67-year old Garrison Frazier, a Baptist preacher and freedman, who had purchased his freedom from slavery. Stanton inquired as to the reaction of the group to be free and how did they think they could best support themselves. The universal answer was land to farm in which they would have ownership.

When it came to the question of what the blacks thought of their treatment by Gen. Sherman, Stanton asked Sherman to leave the room. The clergy answered that they had been received and treated by Sherman as friend and considered him a gentleman. Unanimously they endorsed the general as one who had earned their utmost gratitude. They didn't feel they could be in better hands. In dealing with the man firsthand, they formed an opinion markedly different from the liberals in Washington, less friendly to the general, who had informed President Lincoln that he showed an almost criminal dislike for the blacks.

From this meeting sprang Special Field Order No. 15 calling for many of the coastal islands in Georgia, Florida and

Sherman Takes Savannah

South Carolina to be given to the blacks. This was a vast tract of coastal land confiscated and set aside for black homesteaders. It stretched from the islands south of Charleston and abandoned rice fields on the mainland for 30 miles inland and as far south as all the waterfront lands along Florida's St. Johns River. Whites were barred from these areas. Gen. Rufus Saxton who was serving as Inspector of Settlements and Plantations conveyed the property. To each family would go 40 acres along with clothing, farm equipment and the necessary seed. Obviously it was a popular program and by the summer of 1865 over twenty thousand grants had been made for the former slaves and their families.

The announcement was made at the Second African Baptist Church in Savannah and the response was ecstatic from the assembled crowd. Several hundred blacks attended to hear Gen. Saxon make the decree and announce that as freedmen they were now authorized to occupy abandoned lands along the coastal islands. The order became known as "40 acres and a mule." "You are all free," proclaimed Saxon. "God granted it, Lincoln proclaimed it, and Gen. Sherman has delivered it." After Lincoln's assassination, one of President Johnson's first acts was to rescind the order. Afterwards, strong southern lobbying succeeded in maintaining the status quo.

Sherman was elevated on a plane with Lincoln. Black villages seemed to spring up everywhere on the coastal islands attesting to the program's success. Blacks in the area had a long memory of Sherman and his efforts on their behalf. For the next fifty years they dated events from the time "Tecumsey" was there.

Everywhere Sherman went in Savannah, the black populace mobbed him. They viewed him as their savior and liberator. They were always welcome at his headquarters at the Green mansion and usually visited in droves. He never lost

H. Ronald Freeman

an opportunity to counsel the many blacks that had become camp followers with their new found freedom.

Although he held his tongue at the time, Sherman and Stanton would have no love lost between them for the remainder of their lives. Sherman would never forget Stanton's surprise visit to Savannah and the attitude and pre-conceived notions he brought with him. In fact, during the victory parade in Washington on May 24, 1865, he shook hands with President Johnson and Gen. Grant but declined to acknowledge or shake the hand of Stanton.

Many in Savannah as well as other southern cities didn't care a whit about slavery since their pocketbooks weren't

Foyer of the Green Mansion

Sherman Takes Savannah

directly affected. Their fear was the social equality assumed by northern attitudes would be implanted in the South where the black population was in a majority in many places. Abolition in the southern mind was equated with an equality of the races and given the history of the South, it was just intolerable. Gen. Sherman refused to be drawn into this social ferment. His position was that while he respected local sentiment he felt folks were being influenced more by prejudice than by reason.

It was Sherman's conundrum. No matter what he did it came back to haunt him. As his army tore through Georgia he allowed thousands of the freed slaves to become camp followers and wards of the army. He had been overly charitable even though some of his officers expressed their dislike for having their columns impeded by the followers. He felt his actions had been guided by humanity while Secretary Stanton's was derived from politics.

He had opened his headquarters in Savannah to all the freed slaves and they had come to see him numbering in the hundreds. Many just came to stare at their messiah. He commented he didn't know if he was Moses, Aaron or one of the prophets from the way they looked at him. He encouraged all to behave themselves and be industrious.

H. Ronald Freeman

Occupation

For Savannah, it was over. After four years, the city had succumbed. Savannah had been taken with a cost in killed and wounded of less than 250 even including the losses at Ft. McAllister.

In the 36 days since they left Atlanta for the sea, they had left a black scar through the state some sixty miles wide. With it they left enough bitterness and bad memories to last long after the war. The name of Sherman would become synonymous with pillage and destruction. In taking the war to the citizens he did break their will to continue but also instilled in generations to come a hatred for Yankees that would go far beyond all reason.

The night of Christmas Sherman hosted a dinner at his headquarters in the Green mansion. Turkey and wine were served and he offered a gracious toast and acknowledgement to Green for his hospitality. It is said Green responded to the toast in a very urbane and cultured manner. But did he get his cotton back? No, nor did anyone else. If that had been the motivation for offering his house, it was to no avail.

Sherman's staff found lodging and established their headquarters in private homes in the city for the most part. Gen. Howard's quarters led to controversy after he departed. He chose the imposing town mansion belonging to the British consul. Its previous owner was southern general Henry R. Jackson who had scouted Ft. Pulaski before its seizure by state militia in 1861on Gov. Brown's orders.

Sherman Takes Savannah

Edmund Molyneaux's being British consul did not insulate his residence from appropriation for use as Gen. Howard's quarters. Although Howard was described as a paragon of virtue his staff seemed to fall prey to many of the other vices. Apparently much of the wine cellar and liquors were either consumed on site or "tucked away" for later. Many of the books in the library were "checked out" never to be returned. The Union troops' attitude was that they had little respect for the British government and that applied also to any of their representatives.

Although Molyneaux was British he was also a cotton dealer and a large quantity of his cotton was under federal

Christmas Dinner at the Mansion

confiscation. He demanded its return and Sherman refused. Sherman informed the consul that the British would be treated the same as the Americans.

If the consul had known Sherman's true feelings about the Brits he probably wouldn't have approached him in the first place. Sherman said he was unwilling to fight for cotton for the benefit of Englishmen openly engaged in smuggling arms and instruments of war to kill them. He also said that when the rebellion was over he would be happy to lead a reunited north and south on an invasion of England. He felt there was not a man in his army that wouldn't eagerly join him.

After the army departed, Molyneaux filed a claim against the U.S. for $11,000 in for damage to his home and the loss of books and expensive wines and brandies. He claimed his house had been ransacked. Although many of the missing items did in fact appear later in Union possession, the retort was that Molyneaux was a subject of Britain that sided with the South and the U.S. had no respect for that government or its consul in this country.

Savannah's white population numbered about 20 thousand at the time of its capture. Many of the beautiful squares became camps for the rank and file. Numerous temporary wooden shacks were constructed so that the parks took on the appearance of shantytowns.

The marshal law impressed on the town was necessary to keep order among the Union troops as well as the riff-raff citizens who were prone to looting and had been active participants before federal troops arrived. For administration the city was divided into two military districts and each of those into five sub-districts. In each district there was an officer placed in charge and an 8 p.m. curfew ordered for the enlisted men.

Those soldiers entering Savannah from camps outside the city were required to carry passes. This requirement calling for those on the streets to be in possession of a pass was

Sherman Takes Savannah

strictly enforced. Soldiers were forbidden to enter private houses.

All in all, the northern army was well behaved. The city was quiet both day and night. Sentries were on duty everywhere, even the houses of ill repute. The impression of many of the soldiers was that Savannah had more whorehouses than anywhere they had been before. One commented that he thought Washington had plenty but Savannah even topped that city.

Sitting at the top of all this law and order was Gen. John W. Geary who had been appointed military commander of the city. He had served as a former governor of Kansas and the first mayor of San Francisco. Standing six feet five inches tall, he was a formidable figure indeed. He was a perfect mix of military and politician and possessed a necessary firmness that was leavened with a degree of tact. He knew exactly what it would take to put the town in order and did it, quietly and effectively. Townspeople were delighted with Geary and his able touch. The streets were clean, property was protected and there was a general sense of comfort and security. He was the right man at the right place at the right time.

Gen. John W. Geary

Citizens of Savannah liked and respected Geary.
Under his administration the town was quiet and the town was orderly. When he left in January 1865, the town felt the loss

personally. A resolution was passed by City Council recognizing him as a high-toned gentlemen and a chivalric soldier. Geary responded his only motives were to conduct himself as a soldier but carrying out that charge with deference to charity and humanity.

The men chosen to act as guards of private property were carefully screened to eliminate rowdies, toughs and drunks. A feeling of security and contentment quickly fell over the city. Schools were reopened and operated without incident. Churches were filled on Sunday and business was carried on as it was before the occupation. Sherman was probably right when he wrote in his memoirs, "I doubt if Savannah, either before or since, has had a better government than during our stay."

The city once again came to life. With the river cleared, commerce on the waterfront was brisk. It was as if the clock had been turned back to before the war. The only difference was rather than using slave labor; there was now a stream of blue clad soldiers carrying goods from the docks up the ramps to the city. Daily parades became common accompanied by marching bands. Schools in the city were again in session and local churches were open and filled on Sundays.

Sherman had said at the outset that he wouldn't be responsible for feeding the citizens. After four years of the blockade off the coast, most were starving. However his human side relented and he instructed his commissary to supply food to the needy families of the town. Many citizens came forward to take an oath of allegiance to the U.S. although most had no love lost for the Union. Some were truthful. Henry F. Willink, Jr. who built the southern gunboats *Savannah, Georgia, Macon* and *Milledgeville,* didn't deny his southern sentiments at his hearing. The presiding officer was so impressed with his honesty, he recommended his release.

It was undeniable that the city was sick of war. Its

Sherman Takes Savannah

mayor, Dr. Richard Arnold, was well aware of the outcome of the struggle and decided to seek ways to lessen unnecessary bloodshed. He also knew if the struggle continued, the South would be subjected to a harsher settlement by the victors. He told his fellow Confederate diehards, "Where resistance is hopeless, it is criminal to make it."

Citizens of Savannah were obviously wondering what was going on now that they were occupied and how they would be affected. They petitioned Mayor Arnold for a public meeting that was held the night of December 28th. It was estimated it was attended by in excess of 700 residents.

Mayor Arnold opened the meeting and announced to the assembled body that based on the reality of the situation he could only recommend one course of action. The mood was one of defeat. As a body they voted to put an end to hostility and again submit to the U.S. Constitution. This was in accordance with President Lincoln's amnesty proclamation.

For Savannah, the war was over. After four long years, Savannah was officially at peace with the United States and as such no longer an active participant in the war. It was hard to say what the deciding factor was. It may have been that seeing the Yankees up close and personal, they observed that they weren't the ogres they had been painted.

A general vote was held with citizens agreeing to submit to the national authority. Others who wished to leave were permitted to do so and escorted under a flag of truce to either Augusta or Charleston since those two cities were still in southern hands. Many of the families of Confederate soldiers accepted the offer.

Not to anyone's surprise, Savannah's action didn't play well in other cities in the South. Comments like, "'a crying shame', 'most disgraceful', 'those miserable sycophants'" and others came flowing back. Many cities felt Savannah's action would encourage other southern towns to follow suit.

Regardless, there were immediate benefits to again pledging allegiance to the federal government. The populace was awash in Confederate money that had no practical value as currency to purchase any of the necessary goods such as food or fuel. Fortunately, Sherman turned over to the civil authorities the food supplies left behind by the retreating Confederates.

Massive amounts of supplies and food were coming into town and locations were being sought for their storage. Sherman wanted his army well fed and rested. Confederate money was already considered worthless and when some had been found outside a printing office by the occupying federals and offered by the handfuls to the residents for food and services, they declined.

The biggest problem now was feeding the throng of freed slaves that had stampeded into the city as the federal army advanced and now the town was awash with them. This group swelled the normal population that for more than a month had been on the verge of starvation. A large portion of the food supplies left by the Confederates was rice that in itself could be used as a medium of exchange for purchasing foodstuffs in the North. It seemed to be a good trade. The storehouse totaled about 50 thousand bushels valued at an estimated 265 thousand dollars.

* *

Sherman asked the city council to appoint a committee to oversee the sale of rice in the North. About this same time a Polish messiah, in the name of Julian Allen from New York, appeared in Savannah. Allen was a crusader who had already amassed a comfortable fortune for himself in tobacco and real estate. Being Polish, Allen identified with Count Pulaski of Revolutionary War fame who was one of the heroes of the Siege of Savannah in 1779. He was accepted immediately by

Sherman Takes Savannah

the Council and Sherman to act as Special Agent in the sale of rice for other products in New York.

Allen returned north and became an eloquent champion for Savannah's poor and undernourished citizens. His targets were both New York and Boston. Allen decided to only sell the rice as a last resort. Rather, he would appeal to the generosity of his fellow merchants asking them as a gesture of goodwill to send food to the stricken city. He appeared before the New York Chamber of Commerce and made an impassioned plea. He waved a copy of the loyalty resolution signed by Savannah on December 28th and painted a glowing picture of the city's loyalty to the Union.

What he was seeking, he said, was noble charity for a fallen and repentant foe. Charity for the weak and starving women and children who raised themselves from their pallets to cheer weakly but fervently for the old flag as it passed. It was a long and moving speech and enthusiastically applauded. Resolutions were passed asking for public subscriptions.

Edward Everett

The next morning the *New York Times* and other metropolitan papers gave editorial approval to the idea. The *Times* called on all good men to come to the aid of the stricken foe. New York's Chamber of Commerce tacitly endorsed Allen's proposal

H. Ronald Freeman

although many members dissented and expressed opinions that the only way to coax southerners back into the Union was through sharp steel and cold lead.   In spite of this sentiment New York responded generously.

Shortly, subscriptions began to pour in to the Chamber's committee, some as high as thousands of dollars and some as low as five dollars. Cargo vessels *Daniel Webster* and the *Rebecca Clyde* were donated by a steamship company for the provisions when ready to sail.

Four days after his speech in New York, Allen presented his case to Boston merchants in Faneuil Hall to a gathering of large attendance. He made his appeal quoting the parable of the prodigal son from the Bible. He was merely an opening act though for the main speaker of the evening. This was none other than Edward Everett, the noted orator who preceded Lincoln at Gettysburg.

Everett said let us not strike a business deal but offer the goods to them freely. Not in the spirit of almsgiving but as a pledge of fraternal feeling. It was the old statesman's last great speech. The exertion of delivery was too much and he died within the week. The meeting ended with a hearty endorsement of Allen's plan and three cheers for Sherman and Savannah.

Within three days $33,541 dollars had been raised, $2,000 more than New York had accomplished in the same period of time. The gifts varied in size from $2,500 to a dollar given by three young boys from New Bedford. Even P.T. Barnum, the showman, made the list with a contribution of 50 dollars.

The majority was spent to outfit the *Daniel Webster* and the balance to provide a cargo for the *Greyhound,* sailing from Boston with Col. Allen and representatives of the Boston committee aboard.

The *Rebecca Clyde* sailed on the 14th of January. She carried 970 barrels of flour, 428 barrels of cornmeal, 47 boxes of bacon, 15 boxes of ham, 5 boxes of shoulders, 5 cases of

Sherman Takes Savannah

lard, 100 sacks of salt, 21 barrels of pork, 15 barrels of beans, 6 drums of codfish, 407 bags of potatoes, 10 boxes of onions, 60 bags of pilot bread, 150 quarters of beef, 100 sides of sheep, 25 barrels of molasses, 10 barrels of pickles, 10 barrels of vinegar, 20 boxes of mustard, 6 boxes of pepper and 5 kegs of bicarbonate of soda. She arrived in Savannah on the 19th.

The *Daniel Webster* sailed the next day, her cargo being purchased primarily by Bostonians. On January 9th, the same day Sherman started his army moving to the Carolinas, the *Rebecca Clyde* anchored below the city. The following day she was joined by the *Daniel Webster* and the day after, the *Greyhound* with Col. Allen and members of the Boston committee aboard. The committee presented a letter to the Mayor and Council of Savannah from Mayor Lincoln of Boston. The letter stated that Boston was proud to reopen an ancient and profitable trade that existed between the two cities. It was also a chance for Boston to show her appreciation for Savannah being willing to come under the protection of the Constitution again.

Citizens for Food

Moreover there were historic ties binding the two cities together. They remembered the earlier kindness and liberality

H. Ronald Freeman

of the citizens of Savannah toward the people of Boston during the dark colonial days. "We remember the meeting held there on the 10th of August 1774 when a committee was appointed to receive subscriptions for the suffering poor of Boston. There were large donations of rice to relieve the hunger due to the British closing the port. In memory of past days, of common dangers and common suffering of a united people struggling to be free stands before us." The debt had been repaid. Also generous in donating a cargo of goods was the city of Philadelphia.

A meeting was held at the Cotton Exchange to determine how the food should be distributed. The rub came with who would unload the largess from the ships. The most memorable problem with the ships and supplies coming to Savannah were the citizens themselves.

They asked Sherman's commissary chief to assign some Union soldiers to unload the ships on their behalf. The request fell on deaf ears since the Vermont native had his own opinion as to what slavery had done to the industry of the people. He threw them out, not believing that the men were unable to work to receive a gift to which they weren't entitled. He was enraged attributing the request to their lazy attitudes based on having slaves to obtain their every need. As a result, local laborers were retained to unload the ships.

Gen. O.O. Howard

A New York correspondent who had come in with the flotilla of mercy described the scene for his paper. "Rome, in time of the carnival, can exhibit no greater spectacle. There are two doors to the store, one on Bay Street and

Sherman Takes Savannah

the other on Barnard Street, affording entrance and exit.

Hundreds of people of both sexes, all ages, sizes, complexions, costumes; gray-haired old men with bags, bottles and baskets; well dressed women wearing crepe for their husbands and sons, who have fallen while fighting against the old flag, with pale and sunken cheeks, stand there patiently awaiting their turn. There are women with tattered dresses - old silks and satins. It is a ragman's affair. There are old dilapidated wagons, pulled by weak and broken down horses with rope harness. There are also persons who have never known want, who will suffer silently rather than mix in the crowd which throng at the door. It is a motley crowd of several hundred standing in line with their tickets waiting their turn."

* *

There were many families in town that had Union connections and members of Sherman's staff, and Sherman himself in many cases, called on these. The Gordon home received Sherman and many of his staff during their stay in town. Mrs. Gordon was a transplanted Yankee from Chicago with her father and two brothers in the Union army and another in the U.S. Navy. Her husband, however, was southern through and through and a captain in Wheeler's cavalry. Mrs. Gordon's uncle by marriage was Gen. Hunter who had commanded the attack on Ft. Pulaski earlier in the war.

Sherman made an early visit to the Gordon home to deliver a letter from one of her brothers, a Union colonel and a personal friend of Sherman. Another visitor was Gen. Howard who had four small daughters whom he missed terribly. He knew there were two small Gordon girls and looked forward to sharing their company.

The girls took to the general at once and eagerly sat on his knees. Howard was missing his right arm that had been amputated after the battle of at Malvern Hill during the peninsular campaign (the battle of Seven Pines) in 1862. Juliette, called Daisy, who was nine and a few years older than her sister Nelly, immediately noticed the missing appendage and like all children who are so innocent and honest she said, "You have only got one arm." Gen. Howard said he had lost it in a fight with the rebels and replied, "Are you sorry for me?" Daisy said, "I shouldn't wonder if my papa did it. He's shot lots of Yankees." Outspoken little Daisy would grow up to found the Girl Scouts of America.

The week following Christmas Sherman received word that his six-month-old son Charles had died. He had never seen the infant. He learned of his death from a New York newspaper dated December 22nd. He had also lost his first-born son Willy to typhoid fever early in the war.

Gen. Howard asked Sherman if it would be possible to have a few days leave. Apparently Christmas brought a wave of homesickness to all and Howard yearned to see his wife and young children. Sherman refused and said, "I'd give a million dollars, if I had it, to be with my wife and children. Would you do more than that?" Howard acquiesced and said, "I'll say no more."

Captain Gordon received word that his wife was entertaining the enemy in their home and penned a letter to his wife. He said he could accept the enemy in his city and his home since it was a time of war. He did ask that she refrain any socializing that was unnecessary in polite society. Sherman did issue a pass allowing her to visit her husband in South Carolina. Union Gen. William P. Carlin recorded in his memoirs that a very accomplished and agreeable lady of northern birth but southern adoption had procured from Gen. Sherman permission to visit Charleston where her husband was located in the Confederate service.

The Union army's back pay had caught up with them and the men were ready to spend part or all of it on the dissipations that soldiers throughout history have enjoyed. Although gambling was prohibited, dice and card games

Sherman Takes Savannah

sprung up everywhere. Even thoroughbred racing was initiated with captured horses and the betting was furious. Several riots closed the track down for the safety of all. The world's oldest profession was thriving and the ladies quite happy to receive in exchange for their wares some money with value to it.

Savannah families were hard up for federal dollars or "greenbacks as they were called. The army of occupation had pocketfuls. Many household kitchens were employed full-time in baking cakes, cookies and other goodies for the Union troops. The women were skilled bakers and the men constituted a ready market. It was a good exchange. To the dismay of the troops, many Savannah merchants refused to differentiate between worthless Confederate money and U.S. greenbacks.

Sherman was proud of his army and on several occasions paraded it through the city for the residents to see. On Christmas Eve the 15th Corps marched through the streets to parade music and moving with the cadence they remembered from earlier training.

H. Ronald Freeman

For several hours they filled the streets. The following week the other three corps had an opportunity to show their colors. The horses pranced, the bands played and the flags streamed. Many of Sherman's officers said it was the most splendid review of troops they had seen and the general himself confessed it was the best of all.

The recently freed slaves watched the troops with glee. They needed no encouragement. They danced, jumped,

clapped their hands and followed the bands wherever they went. They became an attraction for many of the northern troops, most of whom had never seen black folks. But make no mistake about what was the main attraction, It was none other than "Uncle Billy", as his men affectionately called him. Sherman was decked out in dress uniform on his horse and the streets of Savannah were jammed with onlookers to satisfy their curiosity with a look at the man himself.

Sherman Takes Savannah

Sherman had requested of Mayor Arnold that he instruct the citizens to turn out to witness his army in review. Arnold refused. He told the general that many of these people had brothers, fathers, sons and sweethearts still away fighting for the southern cause and there was no way in good conscience he could order them out to see the Yankees parade. His exact words were, "Sir, I'd be damned if I do."

Although there were a few dissenters, most of the northern troops fell in love with the city. Comments ranged from it possessing "every mark of wealth, intelligence, refinement and aristocracy," to "being charmed with its beautiful appearance, so different from anything seen before." One correspondent was reminded of the "scenery, grandeur and romance of Italy."

Finally it was time to head north. Early in the second week of January, a steamer transferred two divisions of Gen. Howard's 15th Corps to Beaufort. Also at mid-month two divisions of the Gen. Slocum's 20th Corps crossed the river into Carolina. Several days later a portion of the 14th Corps marched up the Georgia side of the river to Sisters Ferry and crossed there into Carolina. Many of the troops would carry good memories of Savannah for the rest of their lives.

Sherman received a communication from Gen. Grant acknowledging his plan to march his army north wreaking havoc in South and North Carolina before joining Grant in Virginia. Sherman responded with a detailed plan for the invasion of South Carolina. He was ready to again get in the field and leave the city life and politics behind.

Now everything was in preparation for the gathering storm that would descend on Carolina. Gen. Slocum commented that now the state that started all the aggression would be the recipient of it. The tables were being turned. All the might and determination of a well-equipped military machine was heading north to extract retribution. It would be terrible indeed. Even Sherman said, "The march through

H. Ronald Freeman

South Carolina will be one of the most horrible things in the history of the world."

Sherman was glad to leave the city. Putting Savannah behind him would free him from those asking for protection and away from the northern carpetbaggers, already flooding in to seek profits by any means.

Looting in Savannah had been rare but there were memorable cases. Colonial Cemetery was ravaged when the men who camped there began breaking into burial vaults in search of jewelry and silver. A rumor had spread that citizens knowing of Savannah's imminent capture hid their valuables in the family vaults.

The extent of spoiling and desecration was such that many grave markers were never returned to their proper locations and had to be mounted on the eastern wall of the cemetery. Bodies and bones were also disinterred and scattered about. Some tombstone's dates of birth and death were altered for the amusement of those camped there. It was not only in Savannah but also all along the march that marauding Yankees found valuables concealed in family cemeteries.

Maj. Gen. Cuvier Grover of Maine succeeded Gen. Geary as military commander of the city. Even with all the ongoing work cleaning up the city it was still in poor condition. Everything was in a state of disrepair. Houses needed painting and whitewashing. Fences were falling down. In the public sector the streets and sidewalks were cracked and broken where they had been wrecked to provide ballast for the obstructions sunk in the river by the Confederates to block Union boat access. The city docks were sagging into the river in many places. Carcasses from dead horses littered the streets.

Following the departure of the main body of the army, the maintenance department that remained removed 568 animal carcasses, 7,219 loads of manure and 8,311 carts of garbage. A coat of whitewash was applied to the warehouses

Sherman Takes Savannah

on the river and 6,200 trees were whitewashed in a single month.

H. Ronald Freeman

On to Carolina

Sherman's men bore no particular malice toward Georgia, but they felt South Carolina was different, it being the cradle of secession. That state had incited the war and all the destruction that attended it. As one Union soldier wrote, "If we don't scorch South Carolina, it will be only because we can't get a light." That seemed unlikely since it was rumored that Kilpatrick's men had spent five thousand dollars on matches while in Savannah and that every cavalryman's saddlebags were filled with them. In Georgia few houses were burned, but in South Carolina, few would be overlooked.

Sherman, and many of his officers and troops, looked forward to exacting revenge on the Palmetto State, birthplace of the Confederacy and scene of the first shots fired at Ft. Sumter in Charleston Harbor. Sherman said of his march, "I'm

Sherman and his generals
1) O.O. Howard 2) John A. Logan 3) Wm. B. Hazen
4) Wm. T. Sherman 5) Jefferson C. Davis
6) Henry W. Slocum 7) Joseph A. Mower 8) Frank Blair

Sherman Takes Savannah

going to begin marching to Richmond..and when I go through South Carolina it will be one of the most horrible things in the history of the world. The devil himself couldn't restrain my men in that state." They were launching the juggernaut into the Carolinas to make them pay. Having seized Savannah, and undeterred by relentless rain, rugged terrain and sporadic resistance, Sherman ordered his army to move into South Carolina in mid January.

Howard's half of the army was to be placed on ships and transported to Beaufort. The city of Savannah remained occupied by General John Foster and a division sent from Virginia by Grant. In transporting Howard's 17th Corps, for nine days the boats went back and forth without a hitch. However, soon after the 15th Corps began its move, the heavy rain and choppy water made the embarkation so hazardous that the trips by water had to be abandoned. The remainder of the 15th Corps was forced to march in the gummy mud, biting wind and blinding rain to rejoin their comrades. Once his armies were reunited, Howard feinted toward Charleston and then drove directly toward Sherman's true objective in that state: Columbia, the state capital. Sherman left Savannah and joined them in Beaufort on January 21st.

Leaving Savannah, Gen. Slocum pushed one of his two corps across the Savannah River and then advanced on both sides to threaten Augusta. The two Corps were to reunite at Sister's Ferry near Purysburg and march for Columbia. When Slocum finally reached Sister's Ferry, the river was almost twice its normal width and wildly raging. Attempting a crossing was much too risky so there was nothing to do but wait. At this point his column would be a considerable distance from Howard's, almost fifty miles.

H. Ronald Freeman

Sisters Ferry Crossing

    The weather became Sherman's immediate obstacle and not rebel resistance. It had rained for several weeks, and Carolina's lowlands were flooded. Pontoon bridges were being washed away, and columns could trudge only a few miles a day through the deep mud. Roads were altogether impassable, so sticky and oozing with mud that all movement had to stop. The rain was torrential to the point that the old-time natives admitted they had seen nothing like it in their memory. Creeks and streams flooded their banks and turned the lowlands into raging floodwaters and covered the highways

Sherman Takes Savannah

with several feet of water. While pickets stood duty in boats, men slept in foot-deep water. A newspaper reporter found Gen. Williams and his entire staff among the branches of a large tree like so many chickens.

Sherman's wheeled vehicles numbering 70 cannon, 2,500 supply wagons, and 600 ambulances, were heartily cursed by the

Swamp Crossing

soldiers who had to bring them along through the mud. All this notwithstanding, Howard bridged the streams, corduroyed the remainder of the path, then continued his advance. The Confederates were astounded. Confederate Gen. Joseph E. Johnston said, "There has been no such army since the days of Julius Caesar." Hardee, on the scene, barely believed the evidence of his own eyes.

H. Ronald Freeman

Fire Near the Arsenal

When it seemed it couldn't get worse for the populace in Savannah, it did. Most of the Union troops had already crossed the river into South Carolina. On the night of January 27, about 11 p.m. and without warning, fire broke out on the west side of town.   It started   in a stable next to the Confederate naval arsenal in Granite Hall near Broughton and West Broad (M.L.K. Blvd.) Streets. Several fire companies quickly responded to the scene and organized bystanders to remove ammunition before the flames closed in. An hour after it started it still hadn't been contained and had spread to the arsenal.

      Explosion after explosion was set off. Shell fragments were propelled throughout the city as hundreds of cannonballs and 50 tons of black powder ignited. The resulting fires jumped from building to building downtown and created an inferno of flames and smoke. Many were convinced the rebel army had returned and was mounting a counterattack.

      When it was finally extinguished, estimates were that one to two hundred buildings were destroyed and possibly

Sherman Takes Savannah

seven lives lost. The next morning residents could be seen carrying their few remaining possessions from still smoldering buildings. An area of about six square blocks was burned to cinders. Only singular chimneys remained as sentinels in surveying the aftermath. Exploding shells from the arsenal had been thrown all over the city. Those present described it as a night of horror.

Who was to blame? Each side blamed the other. Was it arson? Was the North or South behind it? Good questions all but all left unanswered. The fire was a fact but the inception remains a mystery. Placing blame for the fire also brings up the oft-asked question of, "Why didn't Sherman burn Savannah as he had Atlanta? The answer seems to lie in logistics. Savannah's port was an invaluable prize as a naval base and supply center. By stationing a federal garrison in Savannah, not only would it solidify the gains made by marching through the state but close the port to anyone daring enough to run the federal blockade and bring supplies in to the Confederacy.

Of the Confederate soldiers who had evacuated Savannah and retreated to Hardeeville, Gen. Hardee retained control of his small army primarily made up of the Georgia militia. A manpower shortage though was not the only problem facing the Confederates. Believing the war was beyond salvation, men were returning home in droves, deserting the Army of Tennessee, the Army of Northern Virginia and state militias. Many responded to pleas from wives and mothers, who had so proudly packed them off to war, now to return and protect their homes.

Sherman had accomplished this disintegration of Confederate morale and military forces, and the effect accelerated as he ravaged the Carolinas. Hardee was instructed to stop Sherman at South Carolina's wide rivers. The rebels were to defend Charleston, but to abandon it if necessary and protect Columbia.

True to his word, Sherman blazed a fiery trail through the Carolinas. He left behind only the ashes and cinders of

H. Ronald Freeman

homes, cotton gins and barns. Residents could only stand by and watch helplessly as those in blue beneath the American flag destroyed their property. They laid waste to much of the state where the rebellion began and were able to reach Columbia in less than a month.

Columbia Entry

Like Atlanta, Columbia was substantially burned on February 17th and 18th. Southerners blamed Sherman for setting the city ablaze, although the fire seems to have begun among cotton bales lit by retreating Confederate cavalry under

Sherman Takes Savannah

Wade Hampton before the federal army ever reached the city. Apparently they torched the area's cotton to keep it from falling into Yankee hands. Perhaps they remembered the chastising Gen. Hardee received from the Confederate Congress for letting cotton in Savannah be captured by the Union.

Sherman denied his part in the burning but said, "Though I never ordered it, and never wished it, I have never shed any tears over it. I believe that it hastened what we all fought for, the end of the war."

News of Sherman's triumphal march through Georgia and Carolina provoked unwarranted criticism of his commander Gen. Grant. While Sherman was piercing through the deep South, Grant was depicted as the dull, unimaginative general who was content to do nothing other than remain facing Lee's front.

There was talk of promoting Sherman equal to Grant's rank. He would have none of it and wrote to his brother John, who was now one of the most influential men in the Senate, that he would decline any such promotion if offered. "I have all the rank I want," he told a friend in jest. "Grant stood by me when I was crazy and I've stood by him when he was drunk and now we stand by each other always."

H. Ronald Freeman

Sayler's Creek

During this period, Lee's dwindling army was in constant retreat and being decimated at every turn. Rations and supplies had run out. The Savannah Volunteer Guards, in it from the first when they participated in the capture of Ft. Pulaski at the war's outbreak, were also in it at the last. Their ranks too had withered and been pared down by battles and disease. The unit's last fight was at Sayler's Creek, Virginia, April 6, 1865. Not only were they out of food but out of shot and powder as well. Just before Appomattox, commanded by Maj. William S. Basinger of Savannah, the unit fought a desperate rearguard action.

     The order came down to charge, "Bayonets Forward, Double-Quick, March!" In laymen's terms this meant affix bayonets and run like hell in a screaming charge of desperation at the enemy. The men were willing and they executed as one body. "Theirs was not to question why, theirs was but to do - and die." The fighting was violent and soon broke down into a

Sherman Takes Savannah

series of individual hand-to-hand combat encounters. At the charge there were only 85 men left in the unit. During the charge 30 were killed and 22 were wounded. The few left were taken as prisoners when Gen. Ewell was forced to surrender.

Maj. Basinger too was wounded and captured. They were bowed but not broken, not then not ever. Basinger returned to the battleground after the war and personally paid for the exhumation of his fallen comrades and their return to Savannah where their remains were claimed by relatives. Eleven soldiers went "unclaimed" and were buried together in the Confederate section of Laurel Grove. The statue "Silence" watches over them all.

On April 14th, Lincoln was assassinated at Ford Theatre in Washington. A mass gathering of mourning was held in Savannah in Johnson Square with four to five hundred in attendance. The mood was solemn with surrounding buildings draped in black and church bells tolling. Gen. Grover, his staff and city officials were present atop a large raised platform. The expression of sentiment was that it was with regret that the president was not able to see the reunification for which he had labored so hard - one flag, one country, one people.

Although the fight was still in the men, the means were just not available. That left only one option. Three days later, Gen. Lee met with Gen. Grant at Appomattox Courthouse in Virginia and surrendered his army. Two weeks later in North Carolina, Gen. Johnston surrendered his army at Durham Station, North Carolina. to Sherman. The Confederacy was history. Its period of advocacy and defense of those opinions was over. It was a thing of the past.

H. Ronald Freeman

Epilogue

The bitter reality of Union occupation set in when Sherman's army departed. Gen. Grover succeeded Gen. Geary as military commander of the city but was not cut from the same cloth as Geary. A prime example was presented in March as another bitter pill for the people to swallow. Grover was a stern taskmaster and began enforcing a longstanding order that all women whose husbands were in the Confederate service must be transported beyond existing battle lines. Confederate wives would be escorted outside the city. Gen. Sherman had wisely ignored the order while he was in Savannah. Grover didn't and sent many upriver to Augusta that was still in Confederate hands.

Cuvier Grover

Although again Sherman was the one to receive the criticism for this, he was not to blame. While he was in Savannah he refused to execute this order that came down from higher up. It was only when Grover came to town that the order was enforced. Savannahians remembered this for a long time.

As much as the city liked Gen. Geary, Grover was at the opposite end of the spectrum. In addition, everything about the city was in decay. There were no jobs, no money, the docks were deserted and decaying, the warehouses were

Sherman Takes Savannah

closed and any semblance of commercial enterprise was nowhere to be seen.

One exception was the hotels and boarding houses. They were jammed with northern dignitaries and functionaries and carpetbaggers who came down to make a quick profit at the expense of what they felt were poor ignorant southerners.

In March the black troops arrived to garrison the city. Although they were well behaved, their presence alone was distasteful to the white population. The newspaper ran an opinion to stave off any potential friction. It said, "These black troops are here in this city as United States soldiers, sworn and enlisted to defend and uphold the Constitution and enforce the laws of the United States Government, and as such all parties are bound to respect their uniform, even if they do not the men clothed in them, no matter what their complexion may be."

How effective was Sherman's destruction of crops and rail lines against the southern armies? After all, this was one of his primary goals.

"It was starvation, just literal starvation," said Confederate general John B. Gordon, himself a Georgian, in describing the Army of Northern Virginia's winter months in early 1865 in Petersburg's fetid trenches. Sherman had destroyed vast amounts of food, much of it intended for their use. Worse yet was the ruin of the railroad network in the deep South and it became physically impossible to transport food to Lee. The starving Confederates manning those cruel pits at Petersburg were freezing in threadbare uniforms and bare feet, munitions were barely replenishable. Sherman's unrelenting assault on the Confederacy's civilian sector was largely responsible for that situation.

As the Confederate troops headed for home, few looked like the dashing men in uniform that paraded so proudly at the outbreak of the war. The Chatham Artillery that had seized Ft. Pulaski early on carried with them trunks of clothes, whiskey, and old wines and in some cases their personal butlers. Now,

H. Ronald Freeman

the few that were left were barely recognizable. Skinny, barefoot and ragged as scarecrows, they constituted a pathetic lot.

These ragamuffins began to drift back to Savannah in May 1865. Even there, with the war now over, there were problems. Most returning had nothing to wear other than their uniforms and they were forbidden to wear their Confederate buttons or either made to cover them with black cloth. The men were too proud and opted to cover the buttons rather than remove them.

Savannah had lost its heart and soul and as such was a new place. There was an upheaval of the social order. The former rich were now poor and the city was filled with northern aspirants to newly found wealth. The South had fought the great fight but reality had finally overtaken it. The North had too many men, supplies, boats and munitions. In the end the South had been ground into the dirt. They had fought harder and longer than anyone would have guessed but they had been lockstep to destruction from the first volley of the war.

Sherman returned to Savannah briefly the first week in May to oversee the distribution of food and clothing to civilians. He attended a performance at the Savannah Theatre and as he entered he was greeted by spontaneous cheering until he reached his private box. It was a fitting acknowledgement of his humanitarianism and treatment of the citizens of Savannah.

After the war, Gen. Sherman was promoted to full general and commander-in-chief of the army. He retired from active service in 1884 and lived in New York City from 1886 until his death in 1891.

Reconstruction showered violence on Savannah like her sister cities across the South. Northern carpetbaggers and southern scalawags were prevalent in attempting to take advantage of a defeated society in turmoil. The emergence of the Ku Klux Klan and offsetting organizations for the newly freed slaves escalated the clash of the newly freed with the resentful whites.

Sherman Takes Savannah

The election of 1868 would prove to be bloody in Savannah. U.S. Grant, the northern general, was the Republican candidate and there was a concerted effort among the whites to keep the newly freed slaves from voting. Black whippings and beatings were commonplace. It would be the first time the freedmen would go to the polls to cast a ballot. It all seemed to culminate at the courthouse on Wright Square in Savannah.

A group of white railroad workers went to vote and attempted to force their way ahead of a group of blacks waiting to cast ballots. The blacks refused to be pushed. Police were called. The railroaders said they needed to vote in order to get back to work. The police supported them and they too attempted to push through the blacks. In short order there was a full-scale riot with gunshots, knives, clubs and fists. The encounter resulted in two police officers and two blacks killed. Five other blacks were also wounded.

Joseph Wheeler, commander of southern cavalry, was captured in Conyers near Atlanta after being active in fighting against Sherman's army in the Carolinas. He was imprisoned for only about a month at Ft. Delaware and released. After the war Wheeler entered private business, then won eight terms from Alabama to the United States House of Representatives. When the Spanish American War broke out, he joined the United States Army and led a division of cavalry against the Spanish in Cuba. This time he wore khaki. His service became the symbol of a reunited nation and fulfilled Sherman's belief that if America fought a foreign nation, "Joseph Wheeler would be the man to command the cavalry of our army." Wheeler retired from the army as a brigadier general. He died in Brooklyn in 1906 and was buried with full military honors in Arlington Cemetery.

Gen. Johnston, a Virginia native, settled in Savannah after the war. He had seen the war from its inception at Bull Run to the ultimate surrender in North Carolina. The army he

H. Ronald Freeman

surrendered there was larger than Lee's. In 1868 he entered the insurance business representing the Liverpool and London and Globe Insurance Company. By 1872 the company boasted of more than 120 agents in Georgia, Alabama and Mississippi. During this period Johnston posed for a portrait with Robert E. Lee when he came through Savannah in 1870. He moved back to his native state in 1876, residing in Richmond, and served as a congressman from Virginia from 1879 to 1891.

Gen. Johnston was an honorary pallbearer at Gen. Sherman's funeral in 1891. The old adversaries had kept in touch and had much respect for each other. Johnston, even though 82 years of age, marched bareheaded. The weather was nasty and his friends insisted he cover his head but he refused. He said, "If I was in his place, and he was standing here in mine, he would not put on his hat." True perhaps but also costly. Johnston caught a cold that worsened and he died a little more than a month later on March 21st. He was buried in Green Mount Cemetery in Baltimore.

Gen. McLaws also entered the insurance business, but in his native city of Augusta. He continued in that business until 1875 when he was appointed collector of internal revenue in Savannah. The following year he was appointed Postmaster of Savannah and served two terms. He died in 1897 and was buried in Laurel Grove Cemetery in Savannah.

Gen. Alexander Lawton recovered from a serious wound at Antietam to become Quartermaster General of the Confederacy. He served in that capacity until the ultimate surrender at Appomattox and returned home to Savannah to continue his law practice. He served in the Georgia legislature from 1870 to 1875 and was appointed minister to Austria in 1887. Lawton died in New York in 1896 and was buried in Bonaventure Cemetery in Savannah.

After the war, Gen. Henry R. Jackson also resumed his law practice in Savannah. In 1885, he was named as U.S. Minister to Mexico. He too is buried at Bonaventure Cemetery.

Sherman Takes Savannah

Commodore Tattnall surrendered along with Johnston's army. After the war he too returned to Savannah and served in the post of port inspector that was created especially for him. He died in 1871 on Valentine's Day and was buried in Bonaventure Cemetery.

Gen. Hardee also surrendered with Johnston's army in North Carolina. After the war he moved to Selma, Alabama where he was named president of the Selma & Meridian Railroad. He received a pardon, as did many of his fellow officers, after his old opponent Gen. Sherman endorsed his request. He continued to visit his relatives in Savannah after the war. He died in 1873 and was buried in Selma.

Savannah like her sister cities in the South realized through hindsight their shortages in men and material to wage a war against an industrialized and populated North. Animosity would continue between the two sections of the country even into later generations that had no active involvement in the struggle. What started the war? Was it about slavery and restraining its spread to western states? Or, was it about states' rights and constitutional questions involving the powers granted to the federal government? These questions would be argued by scholars for long periods after the close of the war.

Finally it was over. As one proud returning soldier in Savannah told his wife, "We fought our hearts out but we just got beat." What started with bonfires, speeches and fanfare, ended in the cold reality of war and defeat. From the confusion and first blush of excitement at the Battle at Bull Run to the cold and muddy trenches of Petersburg, the glory in the lost cause was missing.

The economy of the South had to change. Its agrarian practice based on the plantation system and cheap labor was dead. A large segment of its population had been declared to be free but without direction or the means to be productive members of society or self-reliant. Change was necessary and change was in the wind but in the pause of the moment, the

South was rudderless. Like the Phoenix, it would indeed rise from its ashes, but the journey would be long and quite painful.

The End

Sherman Takes Savannah

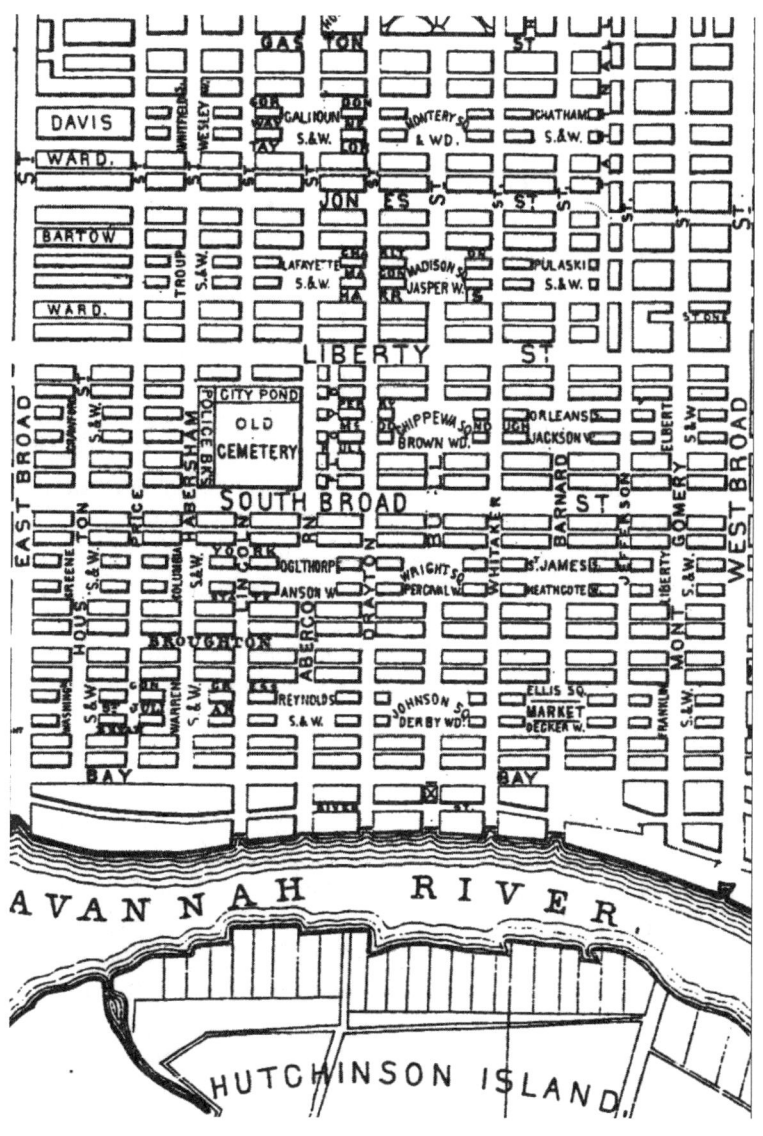

H. Ronald Freeman

Illustrations

1	Johnson Square Oratory	Harper's Weekly
1	Gov. Joseph E. Brown	Library of Congress
1	Harper's Ferry Attack	Harper's Weekly
1	Alexander Lawton	Georgia Historical Society
1	Alexander Stephens	Harper's Weekly
2	Troops Shipping Out to Va.	Leslie's Illustrated
2	Coastal Savannah Area	R.R. Donnelley & Sons, Inc.
2	Josiah Tattnall	Georgia Historical Society
3	Savannah Evacuates	Leslie's Illustrated
3	Robert E. Lee	Julian Vannerson
4	CSS Georgia	Leslie's Illustrated
4	CSS Atlanta	National Archives
5	Francis S. Bartow	Georgia Historical Society
6	Ft. Pulaski	Ft. Pulaski Nat'l Monument
6	Quincy A. Gillmore	Harper's Weekly
6	Plan of Attack on Ft. Pulaski	Harper's Weekly
6	Charles Olmstead	Georgia Historical Society
6	Ft. Pulaski under fire	Leslie's Illustrated
6	John Pemberton	US Military History Institute
6	Damage to Pulaski	Ft. Pulaski Nat'l Monument
7	David Hunter	Civil War Dictionary
8	Ft. McAllister	Georgia Encyclopedia
8	The Montauk	Harper's Weekly
8	John Worden	The Mariner's Museum
8	Montauk destroys Nashville	Leslie's Illustrated
8	Ft. McAllister Map	New York Daily Tribune
10	Henry W. Slocum	Archives of Atlanta Historical Society
10	Peter Osterhaus	National Park Service
10	Frank Blair	National Archives
10	Alpheus S. Williams	National Archives
10	Pontoon Bridge	Library of Congress
10	The Bummer	National Archives
11	Sherman as a Young Man	Library of Congress

Sherman Takes Savannah

11	Sherman	Library of Congress
12	Joseph E. Johnston	Archives of Atlanta Historical Society
12	John Bell Hood	Confederate Portrait Gallery
13	George Thomas	Library of Congress
13	Making Georgia Howl	Harper's Weekly
13	Neckties	Battles and Leaders of the Civil War
13	Braxton Bragg	Illustrated History of the Civil War
14	Joseph Wheeler	Archives of Atlanta Historical Society
14	Hugh Judson Kilpatrick	Library of Congress
14	Millen Prison	Harper's Weekly
15	William B. Hazen	National Archives
15	Storming McAllister	Harper's Weekly
15	Clearing McAllister of Mines	Leslie's Illustrated
17	William J. Hardee	Library of Congress
17	Richard Taylor	Library of Congress
17	Lafayette McLaws	Georgia Historical Society
18	Pierre G. T. Beauregard	National Archives
19	Evacuation	Harper's Weekly
19	Cotton on the Wharf	New York Historical Society
20	Explosion of CSS Savannah	Harper's Weekly
20	Pulaski House	Georgia Historical Society
21	The Green Mansion	Armstrong Atlantic University
21	Christmas - Green House	Harper's Weekly
21	John White Geary	Library of Congress
21	Edward Everett	Harper's Weekly
21	Citizens Awaiting Food	Frank and Marie T. Wood Print Collection
21	Oliver Otis Howard	Archives of Atlanta Historical Society
21	Union Parade on Bay	Harper's Weekly
22	Jefferson C. Davis	National Archives

H. Ronald Freeman

22	Edwin M. Stanton	Notable Names Database
22	Foyer of Green Mansion	Leslie's Illustrated
23	Sherman and his Generals	Library of Congress
23	Sister's Ferry Crossing	Harper's Weekly
23	Swamp Crossing	Harper's Weekly
23	Fire Breaks Near Arsenal	Leslie's Illustrated
23	Columbia Entry	Harper's Weekly
24	Cuvier Grover	Harper's Weekly
24	Volunteer Guards at Sayler's Creek	Keith Rocco
	Map of Savannah	Georgia Historical Society

Sherman Takes Savannah

Bibliography

Bailey, Anne J., *War and Ruin: William T. Sherman and the Savannah Campaign,* The American Crisis Series: Books on the Civil War Era, No. 10, Scholarly Resources, Inc., Wilmington, DE, 2003.

Cox, General Jacob D., *Sherman's March to the Sea,* Da Capo Press, New York, 1882.

Davis, Burke, *Sherman's March,* Vintage Books, A Division of Random House, New York, 1980.

Dyer, John P., *Northern Relief for Savannah During Sherman's Occupation,*

Fellman, Michael, *Citizen Sherman: A Life of William Tecumseh Sherman,* Random House, New York, 1995.

Fraser, Walter J., Jr., *Savannah in the Old South,* The University of Georgia Press, Athens and London, 2003.

Gamble, Thomas, *The Gamble Collection,* Live Oak Public Library, Savannah, Georgia.

Gibson, John M., *Those 163 Days: A Southern Account of Sherman's March From Atlanta To Raleigh,* Coward-McCann, Inc., New York, 1961.

Glatthaar, Joseph T., *The March to the Sea and Beyond,* Louisiana State University Press, Baton Rouge, 1985.

Hart, Liddell B. H., *Sherman: Soldier - Realist - American,* Da Capo Press, New York, 1993, Originally Published Boston: Dodd, Mead & Co., 1929.

Kennett, Lee, *Marching Through Georgia,* HarperCollins, New York, 1995.

Kennett, Lee, *Sherman: A Soldier's Life,* HarperCollins, New York, 2001.

Jones, Charles C. Jr., LL.D., *The Siege of Savannah,* Joel Munsell, Albany, N.Y., 1874.

Jones, Charles C. Jr., LL.D., *History of Savannah, Georgia,* D. Mason & Co., Syracuse, N.Y., 1890.

Lawrence, Alexander A., *A Present for Mr. Lincoln: The Story*

of Savannah From Secession to Sherman, Ardivan Press, Inc. 1961, Macon, Ga., reprinted by The Oglethorpe Press, Inc., Savannah, 1997
Longacre, Edward G., Gentleman and Soldier: The Extraordinary Life of Wade Hampton, Rutledge Hill Press, Nashville, Tennessee, 2003.
Marszalek, John F., *Sherman: A Soldier's Passion for Order,* Vintage Civil War Library, Vintage Books, A Division of Random House, Inc., New York, 1994.
Merrill, James M., *William Tecumseh Sherman,* Rand McNally & Company, 1971.
Miles, Jim, *To The Sea: A History and Tour Guide of Sherman's March,* Rutledge Hill Press, Nashville, 1989.
Nichols, George Ward, *The Story of the Great March,* Harper & Brothers, New York, 1865, Reprinted by Corner House Publishers, Williamstown, Mass., 1972.
Osborn, Thomas Ward, *The Fiery Trail,* 1896-1898. Edited by Richard Harwell and Philip N. Racine, The University of Tennessee Press, Knoxville, 1986.
Schiller, Herbert M., Sumter Is Avenged: The Siege and Reduction of Fort Pulaski, White Mane Publishing Company, Inc., Shippensburg, PA, 1995
Sherman, William Tecumseh, *Memoirs of General W. T. Sherman,* The Library of America, Literary Classics of the United States, Inc., New York, N.Y., 1990.
Smith, Derek, *Civil War Savannah*, Frederic C. Beil, Publisher, Inc. Savannah
Wilson, Adelaide, *Historic and Picturesque Savannah,* Boston Photogravure Company, Boston, Massachusetts, 1889.

Sherman Takes Savannah

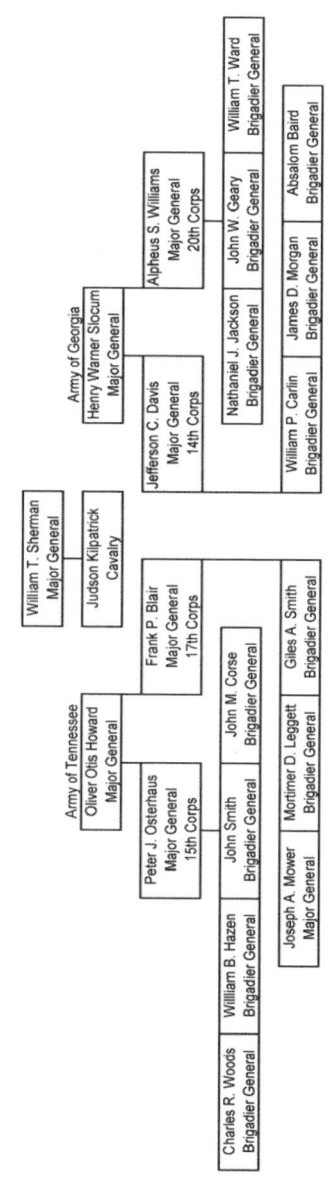

H. Ronald Freeman

Index

Alamo, v, 103, 108, 113
Allen, Julian, 176, 177, 178, 179
Anderson, Edward, 53
Andersonville, 75, 101
Appomattox, 31, 196, 197, 202
Arnold, Richard, 124, 152, 158, 160, 175, 185
Arsenal, 208
Augusta Road, 152, 153
Barnum, Henry A., 152
Barnum, P.T., 178
Bartow, Francis, v, 3, 10, 11, 30, 31, 32, 33, 34, 35, 36, 52, 206
Basinger, William S., 196, 197
Beaufort, 185, 189
Beauregard, Pierre, 32, 33, 34, 54, 65, 93, 94, 95, 103, 129, 130, 131, 141, 143, 144, 145, 148, 151, 154, 207
Bee, Barnard E., 33, 34, 35
Bernard, Simon, 37, 102
Blair, Frank P., 82, 131, 206
Bonaventure Cemetery, 202, 203
Boston, 177, 178, 179, 180, 209, 210
Bowties, 90
Bragg, Braxton, 64, 67, 68, 94, 125, 207
Brent, Thomas W., 154
Brown, John, 1, 77
Brown, Joseph, 4, 5
Bummer, 206
Camp Lawton, 101
Causton Bluff, 53
City Exchange, 36, 152, 153
Clinch, Nicholas B., 112
Cobb, Howell, 92
Cockspur Island, 37, 38
Colonial Cemetery, 186
Columbia, 189, 193, 194, 208

Combahee River, 148, 150
Cox, Jacob, 127, 209
Daisy, 182
Daniel Webster, 178, 179
Davis, Jefferson, 31, 35, 63, 73, 94, 98
Davis, Jefferson C., 83, 130, 163, 207
Davis, Varina, 35
Dred Scott, 1
Dupont, Samuel Francis, 19, 21
Ebenezer Creek, 163, 164, 166
Elliott, Stephen, 9
Everett, Edward, 178, 207
Everglade, 14
Ewing, Charles, 144
Ewing, Thomas, 66
Fingal, 23
Firefly, 149
Foster, John, 120, 125, 138, 189
Frazier, Garrison, 166
Ft. Greene, 37
Ft. Jackson, 12, 13, 52, 53, 146, 154
Ft. McAllister, v, 13, 25, 55, 56, 61, 104, 105, 116, 119, 161, 170, 206
Ft. Moultrie, 5
Ft. Pulaski, v, 6, 7, 11, 12, 18, 19, 20, 24, 26, 38, 42, 43, 45, 49, 52, 55, 106, 161, 170, 181, 196, 199, 206
Gallie, John B., 56, 58
Geary, John W., 83, 152, 153, 154, 155, 173, 186, 198, 207
Gillmore, Quincey A., 39, 45, 48, 49, 50, 206
Gordon, Eleanor Kinzie, 40
Gordon, John B., 199

Sherman Takes Savannah

Grant, Ulysses S., 28, 66, 74, 75, 76, 77, 78, 86, 104, 118, 119, 120, 138, 151, 157, 160, 162, 168, 185, 189, 195, 197, 201
Green House, 207
Green Mansion, 207, 208
Green, Charles, 158
Greyhound, 178, 179
Grimes, Stephen, 112
Griswoldville, 96, 125, 128
Grover, Cuvier, 186, 197, 198, 208
Halleck, Henry W., 69
Halpine, Charles G., 48
Hardee, William J., 64, 67, 103, 108, 116, 118, 119, 120, 121, 125, 126, 128, 129, 130, 131, 132, 133, 136, 137, 138, 139, 141, 142, 143, 144, 145, 149, 150, 151, 152, 154, 156, 157, 158, 191, 193, 195, 203, 207
Hatch, John R., 126, 127, 138
Hazen, William B., 82, 107, 108, 109, 111, 113, 115, 207
Honey Hill, 127, 128, 132
Hood, John Bell, 64, 73, 75, 88, 93, 95, 101, 120, 207
Howard, Oliver Otis, 79, 80, 81, 91, 94, 96, 102, 104, 107, 140, 155, 156, 170, 171, 181, 182, 185, 189, 191, 207
Hunter, David, 40, 44, 206
Hunter, William W., 29
Hutchinson Island, 142
Isondiga, 130, 137, 149
Jackson, Henry Rootes, 6
Jackson, Thomas A., 32, 33, 81
James, 3, 25, 28, 36, 43, 49, 50, 81, 84, 132, 148, 210
Jingle Bells, 36
Johnson Square, 2, 158, 197, 206

Johnston, Joseph E., 32, 33, 35, 64, 73, 131, 151, 191, 197, 201, 202, 203, 207
Jones, Charles C., 131, 209
Kilpatrick, Judson, 79, 93, 97, 98, 99, 100, 101, 106, 141, 188, 207
Ku Klux Klan, 200
Lamar, Gazaway B., 8, 63
Laurel Grove Cemetery, 36, 197, 202
Lawton, Alexander, 5, 6, 7, 10, 11, 53, 101, 102, 202, 206
Lee, Robert E., 1, 17, 18, 26, 38, 39, 40, 43, 54, 66, 74, 75, 78, 83, 86, 88, 98, 118, 119, 121, 124, 128, 131, 133, 138, 157, 195, 196, 197, 199, 202, 206, 209
Lincoln, Abraham, 2, 3, 4, 53, 74, 77, 160, 164, 166, 167, 175, 178, 179, 197, 209
Little Kil, 99
Louisiana State University, 68, 209
Louisville Road, 152
Low, Juliette Gordon, 40
Macon, 91, 94, 96, 125, 128, 140, 150, 174, 210
Mallory, Stephen, 148
McLaws, Lafayette, 121, 131, 132, 134, 139, 145, 148, 202, 207
McPherson, James B., 81
Mercer, Hugh, 133
Merrimac, 24, 25, 26, 49, 56
Milledgeville, 5, 91, 92, 93, 94, 95, 133, 149, 174
Millen, 94, 101, 102, 207
Molyneaux, Edmund, 171, 172
Monitor, 25, 26, 49, 56
Montauk, 56, 57, 58, 59, 60, 61, 206

Mosquito Fleet, v, 22, 42
Mower, Joseph A., 82
Nahant, 61
Nashville, 58, 59, 60, 64, 120, 206, 210
Nichols, George W., 155, 210
Ogeechee Canal, 130, 140
Ogeechee River, 13, 56, 62, 102, 103, 104, 105, 107, 116, 122, 133, 140, 144
Oglethorpe Light Infantry, 7, 30, 31, 32, 36
Olmstead, Charles, 7, 43, 45, 46, 47, 48, 49, 206
Ossabaw Sound, 13, 62
Osterhaus, Peter Joseph, 81, 131, 206
Oysterland, 102
Page, Richard L., 26
Passaic, 61
Patapsco, 61
Pemberton, John C., 40, 45, 54, 206
Pennyworth Island, 142
Pierpont, James, 36
Port Royal, 16, 17, 21, 26, 28, 61, 103, 104, 116, 125, 136
Pulaski House, 158, 207
Purse, Thomas, 36
Rattlesnake, 58
Rebecca Clyde, 178, 179
Resolute, 140
Rice, 102
Russell, Willliam, 15
Sampson, 140
San Francisco, 67, 94, 173
Savannah River, 13, 14, 18, 19, 23, 24, 37, 52, 78, 102, 118, 119, 121, 130, 131, 136, 137, 139, 140, 142, 157, 161, 189
Saxton, Rufus, 167
Second African Baptist, 167
Sherman, Charles, 66
Sherman, William T., 66, 209

Silence, 146, 197
Sisters Ferry, 185
Slocum, Henry Warner, 79, 80, 91, 92, 102, 113, 120, 136, 137, 140, 155, 156, 163, 185, 189, 206
Smith, Gustavus W., 82, 125, 126, 127, 128, 131, 132, 145, 148, 210
Special Field Order No. 15, 166
Stanton, Edwin M., 116, 157, 165, 166, 168, 169, 208
Stephens, Alexander, 8, 206
Stowe, Harriet Beecher, 1
Tattnall, Josiah, 13, 14, 15, 19, 24, 25, 26, 29, 124, 149, 203, 206
Taylor, Richard, 126, 128, 207
Thomas, George H., 32, 36, 66, 75, 93, 104, 154, 207, 209, 210
Toombs, Robert, 5, 126
Totem, Joseph, 39
Traveller, 18
Tybee Island, 11, 13, 18, 19, 20, 37, 39, 41, 42, 45, 46
Uncle Billy, 69, 72, 184
Union Way, 118, 120, 136
Vernon River, 13
Virginia, 1, 25, 30, 32, 39, 56, 66, 74, 75, 78, 83, 86, 98, 119, 120, 121, 124, 132, 133, 137, 138, 157, 162, 185, 189, 193, 196, 197, 199, 201
Walcutt, Charles C., 96
Webb, Willliam A., 26, 27, 28
Weehawken, 26, 27, 28
Wesley, John, 37
West Broad Street, 142, 147, 153
Wheeler, Joseph, 93, 96, 97, 98, 99, 100, 101, 130, 137, 142, 148, 164, 166, 181, 201, 207
White, Thomas A., 104, 207, 210

Williams, Alpheus S., 82, 83, 131, 191, 206
Willink, Henry F., Jr., 174
Wilmington River, 13, 19, 27, 53, 148, 154

Wilson,, James, 43, 44, 210
Worden, John, 56, 206
Wright, Ambrose R., 131, 132, 133, 201